D1521681

Renew and Restore

How To Communicate, Connect and Celebrate Your Best Self

A Personal Development Book

Written by

Patty Mohler, MS, LMHC

Love Notes

"Patty's book is a must-have for anyone looking to improve their communication skills, relationships and become a better human being on this planet. It is chock full of real-world applications, straight-forward explanations and beautifully touching stories of her life. Anyone who picks up this book is a fortunate recipient of Patty's unique ability to boil it all down into heartfelt, useful practices that anyone can benefit from."
~ Dennis and Kathy Lang, International Yoga Teachers~

"The intimate journey through Patty's life exemplifies how we are all kindred souls. She connects life's experiences and how they lay the foundation for our sense of self-worth and how to best grow positively from them. Her journey has led her to help guide us through ours. The writing is bold and brave and genuine. Patty's insight gives us the ability to carve a pathway into our mindset and emerge as our best self."
~Nancy Watson, Watson Realty~

"Patty's book is a fascinating read for anyone looking to improve their communication skills, relationships, and become a better human being. It is chocked full of real-world applications, straight-forward explanations and beautifully touching stories of her life. After reading her book, I am noticing myself and others exhibiting behavior that is *described in the book. Awareness is the first step. Now, with Patty's useful practices, I know how to handle those situations better."*

~B.W.~

"Patty raised the bar when speaking to our community of women at Celebrating Possibilities. From the outset, she captured our senses while traveling through her mindfulness journey and delivered us to our destination in synchronized rhythm for her well-deserved standing ovation. We were connected in song and euphoria. It was an evening to remember."

~Aimee Boggs, VP of Raymond James~

"She's honest and intuitive and presents material that both applies and "hits home" with the personalities involved. I have had nothing but great experiences with Patty! Her motivating energy always leaves me with something to think about!"

~Kerry Orton, BSN RN Ascension St. Vincent's Cardiopulmonary Rehab Manager ~

"Patty demonstrates a number of innate qualities that are necessary in working toward the mental wellness of the public. In addition to her commitment to education, healthcare, and health disparities, she is caring and empathetic, yet strong in being decisive. She works exceptionally well with diverse populations and has a special charisma in engaging individuals and audiences of all types. Her presentations on

Mind Your Health topics are especially engaging and impactful. Patty is dedicated and committed to working in mental wellness across diverse populations with a focus on inclusiveness. Patty is an outstanding presenter and a pacesetter in mental wellness."
~Sharon Wilburn~

"I had the pleasure of working with Patty Mohler as the Licensed Mental Health Counselor at St. Vincent's Ornish Reversal Program. Patty is one of the most skilled and captivating speakers that I have witnessed. Patty is knowledgeable and enthusiastic about health and wellness, both of which are evident in her presentations. Patty is consistently positive, professional, and a team player, making her an asset to any team or organization."
~Kat Pitocchelli, MA, RD/LN, Ornish Program Manager~

"I have had the distinct pleasure to participate in group learning activities and discussions facilitated by Patty. She is engaging and resourceful. She allows participants time to think in order to express themselves comfortably within a safe place. She uniquely identifies those individuals that need additional support and is able to provide the needed support while still engaging the group and moving forward in the discussion. Her ability to "read" a group and change directions to meet the needs of the group is remarkable. I find her personality to be caring, genuine and sincere, which allows participants to readily trust her. Her inspirational and thought-

provoking ideas will encourage anyone to embrace the unknown and step out of their comfort zone."
~Ellen Menendez, Board Member AFSP.

"What a great weekend! We learned new skills, and it feels that we got much closer after this. With the beach right there, sunrises and sunsets were amazing and a big bonus." **~C.S.~**

"Have to admit, I doubted going to a couples retreat, but boy, I stand corrected! One of the best things we've done, just amazing!"
~M.P.~

Dedication

Aman, Bods, Brownie, Abod are some of the names he responds to, but my favorite, by far, is son. Witnessing this magnificent young man grow up has exceeded both my wildest dreams and highest expectations. From the day he came into this world, my life has become an adventure. Beside him in this life's journey, I have learned the meaning of unconditional love, experienced overwhelming joy and sadness, and endured immense frustration and pride. He has fought through adversity and reveled in successes both through participation in sports and in day-to-day life. He demonstrates the purest of love for his friends and family. Through all of this, I am humbled to watch him spread his wings and soar like an eagle. He empowers me to rise to the challenge of being a better mother and a better human. As he navigates his future, I am thrilled to be not only a spectator but his biggest fan. My beautiful son, I dedicate this book to you. You are my champion and my pride and joy.

Renew and Restore

Table of Contents

Renew and Restore

Preface

Life is like a river. This phrase is the ultimate analogy for life. Perhaps I use this analogy because much of my foundation was spent on or near the mighty Truckee River in Reno, Nevada. I have spent countless hours on the Upper Colorado or Deschutes Rivers, creating beautiful memories from fishing, backpacking, or kayaking. Each of these rivers is similar to my life's journey; each has a unique course, different characteristics unique only to them, and no two rivers, like people, are alike. Rivers start as a trickle of air and water-born of earth, just like we do. Rivers start slowly and quietly and learn to crawl in a long meandering fashion before they take off down a hill, eventually building to a roaring, noisy life, pouring down the side of a mountain. We all start slowly and learn to crawl before we walk and talk and then run and yell. There is calm water, whirlpools, rapids, and sometimes the water gets stuck behind a rock. Rivers are full of wonder, beauty, and, most of all, strength - much like you and me! We all reach plateaus in our lives. Rivers slow back down and move leisurely again in some places, even becoming stagnant. Our lives are like that, too. We hit peaks and valleys along the way, but most of the time, we get through by doing the next thing.

My journey is like the river: it has seen peaks and valleys, and I have been stuck behind boulders and basked in full sunshine on calm blue waters. On these pages, you will get to know a bit about me and my approach to life. I look back at the steps that led me through transformations, how I have ebbed and flowed. As a therapist, many people come to me to discuss their stagnant marriages, failed relationships, demanding kids, being newly empty nesters, overbearing bosses, unchallenging careers, death of a spouse, or feeling "lost." People come when there is an *ache,* and they don't know how to heal.

This book is meant to empower, motivate, and inspire you to be your best self. I have included exercises used to help not only myself but my clients, all the while of mixing my story with the stories of others I have met along my journey.

In the Fred Rogers movie, *A Beautiful Day In The Neighborhood*, he says, "Let's take one minute to think about all the people who have loved us into being." It would be difficult to not participate right along with the characters in the movie. My friends from childhood and adulthood have loved me *into being*. I would not be who I am today without the deep, unconditional love from my friends with whom I went to kindergarten, junior, and senior high school. These friends, along with my family and adult friends, have unwavering trust and willingness to stick by me through all my ups and downs. They are my wings and have given me flight. I look at these friendships and offer insights on how to connect with those we love.

Most people want to be seen, heard, and validated. To accomplish this, we need to have strong communication skills as they are the cornerstone in both business and personal arenas. I explore active listening and how it is about patience, deep trust, and new perspectives, which can help solve problems and makes you more approachable. We learn how listeners need not interrupt with questions or comments, how active listening involves giving the other person time to explore their thoughts and feelings. I will look at the advances of digital technology, both the good and bad forms of communication.

Just as a river starts slowly, gains speed along the way, and can sometimes be ferocious, codependency can be just as treacherous if not managed. I examine how boundaries protect us like a river's bank, keeping us safe from encroaching waters that might flood our sense of well-being.

"The real gift of *gratitude* is that the more *grateful* you are, the more present you become." — Robert Holden.

Gratitude brought me from the depths of despair. The art of appreciation opens hearts and keeps us mindful. It teaches us to be content with what we have and where we are in the present moment. It is a gift we give to ourselves for peace of mind. Gratitude is a practice, and once we make it a priority, we are forever changed.

This book is just like a river; it winds along looking at different subjects and areas of life. Several different exercises are placed throughout these pages; some might tempt you to explore further, while others might wait to be visited at a later time. Like a river, it's entirely possible that around the next bend, we run into a rock wall or cascade over a giant waterfall into a pool of dangerous boulders. There's also an equal chance that we will encounter a lovely day on a beautiful stretch of blue water where the fish are jumping and living there is excellent. At times, this thing called the river of life can be incredibly difficult. Still, if you've ever fought the frothing whitewater of the Truckee or Deschutes river, any river, you know that peace, harmony, and a calm stretch of water are just around the next bend. If you remember to take along some fine food and good friends, you will have an excellent time again and again.

Patty Mohler

Chapter 1

Many Rivers to Cross

"Mom, why is dad's closet empty? Where is dad?"

I had spent the summer on the East Coast with my brother and Mom when I was six years old. We spent time visiting relatives and fishing on the Chesapeake Bay with my mom's best friend. Once we arrived home, I ran into my parent's bedroom, hoping to see my dad.

Although I don't remember the conversation, it was explained to me dad no longer lived with us, and that my parents were divorcing. While I thought we were on the adventure of a lifetime, we were giving my dad exit space; we were about to discover a new normal — one with a single mom and a dad I would see occasionally.

The divorce would be the first of many pivotal moments in my life.

The second blow came quickly. On the day of the divorce, my mom, surrounded by friends, shed many tears. Then the attorney called, "Mary, the divorce is done. I need to tell you something else. Earlier today, Don married the woman he had been seeing!"

Imagine that. Divorced and married all in one day. This could only happen in Reno, Nevada!

Everyone experiences change throughout their lifetime; this a given. Some transitions are more complicated than othe some are dealt with immediately, while others are hidden the recess of our minds. While working in the mental heal field, I have come face to face with my history. Most therapi: will need to deal with past traumas, addictions, codependency issues, and learn how to manage our ov mental health. Sigmund Freud suggested, "that a good half every treatment that probes at all deeply, consists in t doctor's examining himself, for only what he can put right himself can he hope to put right in the patient." This is wha known as the "wounded healer," that personality trait th helps all healers connect and treat emotional pain. It can be place of great healing, or it can open wounds that, if I untreated, can cause mental health issues. Acknowledgi and accepting what troubles me has helped me become mc empathetic towards my patients' emotional suffering, as we

There are two choices, avoid them or deal with them. It wa during my 20's I decided to explore my past. During this tin I was asked to revisit my parent's divorce. Perception, wh you are six versus 25, is as different as night and day. It v during this time I realized my self-worth, or should I say t lack thereof! Before this time, I remember thinking little of t "divorce;" it was normal for my brother and me. As a child, t most problematic issue was going from home to home. The was no regular schedule; it was based on if my father want to spend time with us. An unsettled, anxious feeling would rear up on special occasions such as birthdays, Christmas, father-daughter dances, as these "need to show them off" days were essential to my father. Choosing which parent to spend time with was vulnerable and felt "icky." My mom was my heart and soul; she loved me and protected me. It felt like a betrayal to ask to spend time with my dad. Yet, I missed him, too. It felt confusing and unsafe. For years I thought, "Okay, my parents divorced, so did many other people. It wasn't too big of a deal." While working with a therapist, I learned to connect the dots of how my past was affecting my present state of being. In my mind, my parents did not divorce because they didn't like each other or have their own issues. *My father left me*. My father, who had been married previously, had two sons, my half-brothers (a term I dislike; they are my *brothers*). I discovered they were roughly the same ages as my brother and I when they divorced. I believed it wasn't just me, but he didn't like kids this age, and that is why he left. Little brains can conjure up all types of misinformation. The revelation that came out of my work is that I believed people always leave *me*. My therapist helped me understand I had a voice; I had permission to be angry, permission to grieve a childhood without a stable father figure.

Luckily for me, I was able to adjust after he was gone. This, in thanks, is due to my mom. She had many significant strengths and was a fabulous role model. She loved us with every fiber in her body. She taught me how to be strong and independent. She taught me to have a voice. She instilled confidence in me; if I put my mind to it, the world was my oyster, and I could do anything!

The time around the divorce had been a humiliating time for my mom. Reno was a small town, and the whispers were more like thunder clapping. It fueled her own insecurities. She was a people pleaser and did not like being judged, especially by my father. She passed these traits down to me. I would never be allowed to go to my father's house in simple play clothes. Well, unless they were clean, all matched, and we looked "presentable." No way would she ever give him a reason to criticize, "Oh, she has holes in her shoes, or that shirt doesn't match those shorts." That was a big deal for her. This perfectionism created enormous pressure and spilled over well into my teen years and beyond. Every time I got dressed I could hear her saying, "Oh, you don't look right" or "You need to dress a certain way to impress somebody."

I learned to be a people pleaser and a caretaker, both of which are codependent qualities that I would have to deal with later in life and were born in these early years.

I remember when I was in my very early twenties, a girlfriend and I were having a conversation about high school. She had lived with us part-time in her senior year as there was tension

4

and alcohol abuse in her own home. During the conversation, she asked me something about being an adult child of an alcoholic. There was a pause, and she said, "You do know you are one. Right?" My father was a well-known physician in town, and he definitely drank his fair share, but an alcoholic? I had never even heard the term! That was my first awakening to the fact that my dad had an alcohol problem or would be called an alcoholic.

Adults who survived childhood environments where alcohol is in the home continue to experience problems unless they make some life changes. Often the home environment is predictably unpredictable. Arguments, inconsistency, unreliability, and chaos tend to run rampant. Children of alcoholics don't get many of their emotional needs met due to these challenges, often leading to skewed behaviors and difficulties in properly caring for themselves and their feelings later in life. For me, I had to discover what an adult child of an alcoholic was. It plunged me into identifying the co-dependency issues I had and how to resolve them. The process was slow and arduous.

Codependency stems from childhood and is something that I've worked long and hard not only to overcome but to educate others. Later in the book, boundaries, the cornerstone to disable codependency, is examined in more depth. Let me give one example of how it started for me. My mother was one who was consistent about having dinner on the table. Somewhere between 6:00 and 6:30 PM, I knew to be in the house and sitting down when food went on the table.

On the other hand, at my father's house, dinner arrived somewhere around nine o'clock. Alcohol was freely consumed, and we were always told: "dinner's coming." When I was little, I would have tremendous stomach aches because I was starved by nine PM. I remember one time I got the courage to ask for a snack and was told "no" since it would ruin my appetite. This simple act of being told "no" was a building block moment, like many others, that started my codependency, and like a river, they would continue to gain momentum for years to come. I learned that my feelings didn't matter. My needs were dismissed, and I didn't have voice.

At 23, I was living in Colorado teaching high school and suddenly was caught in the teacher crunch and lost my job. (temporally, I told myself) moved back to Reno and went to work for my dad until 'I got my feet on the ground' and could move back to Colorado. During this time, my dad was having marital issues and separated from his third wife. Work and life pressures collided for him. A veil of fog, like a dense, dark blanket, covered him. Sadness and regret replaced rational thoughts and feelings. He no longer could see positive moments or people in his life; he was devastated by recent events and could not see his way through his depressing thoughts.

Yes, I knew he was depressed. I witnessed his spiral into darkness every day. My father was also a great actor. He turned on the happy-go-lucky personality and charm as a means to defend the darkness. I would challenge his friends to how he was behaving, and they didn't notice any of the changes. He was the life of the party; he was jovial and always had a good joke. He wore the mask to keep people at bay. For him, the only way to deal with the crisis he was facing was to end his life.

I had just become engaged to a young man my dad had known for years. He was a professional golfer, and many men at the club supported him with words of encouragement and occasionally financially. My father adored my fiancé. I knew my dad needed help, and my fiancé also knew I needed a break. We went to dinner; this would be the first time away from my dad in weeks, considering I worked with him every day and would visit every night after work. I received a phone call from one of dad's friends after dinner, and the silence was deafening. I knew. I knew something was terribly wrong. We drove to my father's home to find him on the floor, naked and blue. The paramedics arrived shortly afterward, and the scene was out of a movie. As we arrived at the hospital, the next unbelievable moment occurred. I rushed into the emergency room and came face to face with my brother. You see, my brother was on call in the emergency room that night; he would have to try to revive our dad. Hope appeared futile. The news got out quickly, and the waiting room filled with my dad's friends.

They were in shock. Their friend, who was an energy force to be reckoned with, made a sad, deliberate choice. His friends did not see this coming. My family did not see this coming. No one heard me. No one took my warnings seriously. He was a good actor!

Life came to a standstill. He made it through the night but was not out of the woods. Paused. It was as if someone hit the pause button. Time stood still. Mornings turned to nights. Nights turned to days. Days turned to weeks. The weeks grew into months. Weeks turned into years. Tubes and resuscitators kept him alive. The daily vigil of friends began to dwindle, and hope drifted away like an early morning fog; without notice, it was gone. The day came when my brother delivered the news our dad would be in this vegetative state for the rest of his life. Selfish as this sounds, my next thought was, "but who will walk me down the aisle in two months?"

After many conversations with my mom, my brothers, and my fiancé, we decided to proceed with the wedding. My grandmother also helped influence our decision by telling me, "Life is for the living." It was as if I could put my worlds into silos. With help from others, I permitted myself to be happy on my wedding day and honeymoon.

Life, for all of us, had a new normal. For me, I focused on work and being a new wife. My daily visits eventually turned to weekly ones, all the while I was searching for balance, trying to survive in this place of limbo at the hospital and "real" life at home. With life hanging in the balance, daily pressures no longer carried the same weight, and I learned to cherish life. The smallest of moments made me happy. The significant "stresses" appeared insignificant. I learned quickly and well: Life is short, live it well, always trust my instincts, value family, and friends.

How a Brook Turns Into a Raging River

"I don't understand why there are dishes under your bed! Explain this!" said my mom. Shame. Scared. The truth was out, and I was caught red-handed. *I was bad.* "I guess I was hungry, so I got something to eat." In my house, there was a double standard. After dinner, my brother was allowed to have dessert. I recollect a different scenario. *I* was not allowed to have dessert. I had to present myself in a certain way, be a certain weight, so, I could not have treats. I would sneak down to the kitchen after everybody went to bed and have dessert and often hide the dish under my bed. These moments were the beginning of a brook turning into a raging river.

From 16 to 23 years of age, I was bulimic, the non-purging type because purging "was gross!" In the early 70's we knew about anorexia, but we didn't have a name for or talk about what I was doing to my body. Bulimia was not a word anyone was familiar with at the time. There was no help.

For those who don't know, bulimia is an eating disorder where you consume 2,000, 3,000, or even 5,000 calories per sitting. You're just stuffing yourself beyond being satiated and consuming as much food as humanly possible to numb whenever you're feeling, or don't want to feel. There are purging and non-purging types. I was the non-purging, all-consuming- until- it -feels -like -I'm- dying type. Denial was my best friend, and denial helped me never admit I had a problem. Denial kept my secret, and we worked well together. Like my father, I was a good actor.

Throughout college, I suffered in silence, and my relationship with food, which protected me from men, loneliness, and anxiety, became my best friend. This disease protected me from ever having to deal with any emotion. That was my drug of choice; I was a bingeaholic.

When I was 20 years old, living on my own in a studio apartment at Colorado State, bulimia grabbed me and dragged me downstream. The current was swift, and there was nothing to stop the forward momentum. I was going from place to place to pick up food; it was a blackout. There was no memory of picking up the food or eating it. Denial continued to protect me. Just like a leaf that gets stuck behind a rock, I somehow stopped at a bookstore and picked up a book by Richard Simmons. (Yes, the funny guy with curly hair, a headband, and crazy short shorts!) I remember doing this and even at the time, questioned my sanity. "Why am I buying a health/fitness book when I am spinning out of control?" I had no answers. Once at home, I sat down and started reading it, and it was as if a hand came out and slapped me in the face. The book said, **"What you are doing to yourself RIGHT NOW is a slow form of suicide."** "WHAT? Wait a minute; I don't want to die." That's not why I'm doing this.

Why am I doing this?

Remember, there was no help back then because there was no such thing as bulimia (that I knew of). Yet, it was my moment of clarity. I knew there was no one to ask for help; it was up to me to find my way out of these troubled waters. For many years, I educated myself, learned how to give myself grace and compassion. A healthy lifestyle became my mission, my passion. Denial was no longer my friend; elimination of the enemy became my purpose. The goal was to allow me to become healthy-mentally, physically, spiritually.

Looking at the symptoms and how they progressed helped me understand that no one person or thing contributed to my disease. It was the DIS EASE I had with myself. The perceptions as a child were analyzed and explored. What if my parents had a difficult marriage and he didn't leave me? Perhaps my mom did not deny me dessert; maybe, just maybe, it was the discipline for not eating my dinner? I remembered my name, Patty, rhymed with fatty, and I remember being called Fatty Patty at school. The girls at school started talking and comparing body shapes and sizes. Bulimia was a leaf stuck behind a rock in my own mind. It swirled and gained momentum. It couldn't find the freedom to move forward. Instead, more issues attached: depression, anxiety, low self-esteem. It would be years before I was set free.

In the midst of working on myself, my dad's suicide occurred I was getting married in three months. The attempt left him comatose for three years. Dad and my fiancé were excellent friends, mostly due to golf (my fiancé was a professional golfer), so it was equally hard on him. Here we were, two young people, trying to set our life in the right direction. So many different things were happening all at once: life, work preparing a wedding. It created new decisions such as who would walk me down the aisle? How are the invitation addressed: is he referred to in the past since he is still alive What do we tell people? People questioned why I was moving forward with the wedding. It felt like judgment in every direction I turned. Under all the pressure, the bulimia reared its ugly head. I, too, was a good actor. Not even my fiancé knew of my secret. But somehow, I loved my fiancé unconditionally, and that was my hope: that I could help myself. It gave me strength.

Turbulence

There was such self-loathing and lack of confidence in myself I could not understand why I was doing this or how to fix the bulimia. It felt as if I was being carried away downstream struggling to stay afloat amongst all the mud, filth, and debris. It was another crisis that propelled me forward; it was as if I was in the rapids of a mighty river and could not come up for air.

At this point, I owned a fitness studio, which was interesting because why would someone with an eating disorder own a fitness studio? Why would I put myself in a position of wearing leotards and tights when I hated the way I looked? That was the 50-million-dollar question from friends and family. The pressure, at the time, was considerable, but I was also able to take one addiction and use it in another way. My exercising was not out of control, just enough so that I was able to stay under anyone's radar. It was my "healthy" addiction. It was fun, it was healthy, and it helped me survive. I could eat whatever I wanted because I was exercising so much, and I was able to keep myself in check with the food intake. I had a healthy lifestyle, and it allowed me to further my healing.

My next pivotal moment was when my son was born. He was an absolute blessing to us. When he was around ten years old, he received a horrible diagnosis, which came with a possible deadly outcome. I spent four or five years finding the right medical professionals to help him. Luckily, we were able to find the right doctors, and he was able to grow into a fabulous young man. However, about three years after his last surgery, I realized that after 25 years, I no longer had a healthy marriage, and it was time to leave.

Prior to our son's illness, we moved to Australia for three years for my husband's job. The eating disorder (Ed) was under control. I was healthy and permitted myself to do anything! In Melbourne, I started painting pottery for fun. When we came back to the United States, I missed it. About this time, painting studios began to pop up around the country. I went to paint one afternoon and felt energized Realizing I missed being creative, I started painting again. One day I thought, "What the heck am I going to do with all this pottery?" One can only have so much stuff in the house. No telling anyone, I packed up some of my works of art and went downtown and talked to the shopkeepers at ten different stores. Several agreed to put my pieces in their shops and se them, which started a 10-year business, Padi Custor Ceramics. Then the economy crashed, and I was gettin divorced. Now I was at another pivotal crossroad.

About this same time, I was standing in my living room, on th phone with a friend. We were talking about the Empty Nes Syndrome, as her third child was leaving home. She lived in very expensive, well-to-do neighborhood, and I jokingly sai "Well, what are you going to do now?" She told me she wa going back to school to become a PA, Physician's Assistant was in awe. She was doing it to improve her life, to follow dream. She was married, raised her children, and now it w her time. Then about 10 minutes later, my sister in law to me that her 30-year-old son was giving up an excellent job a going back to law school. I remember both of those being about 15-minute phone calls. As I stood in my living room, I started to think, what's your problem? What are *you* going to do? What is stopping me?

The answer was like a ticker-tape in my head - You're too old. You can't do this. It's too late for a career. Then I said, "Those are just excuses." I stood in my living room, and it dawned on me that I could be like a river or be a rock. It has been said that in a contest between a river and a rock, the river always wins. Why? Because the river is willing to follow the natural call of gravity, going over, under, around, or, eventually, through the rock, to its destiny which, as with all water, is to ultimately merge with the ocean. The rock is stuck where it is, relentlessly pushing against the river, resisting the natural flow of water until, over a long enough period of time, it's worn down to a pebble.

I went to the computer to search for graduate schools. I would combine everything I knew. I've been a teacher, an artist, I've owned a health and fitness center. This truly is the Trifecta, right? **Mind, Body and Spirit.** I wanted to be a mental health therapist. I was blessed to go to a fantastic therapist during my divorce, and she helped me understand that I was not insane and how to voice what was best for my son and me. Therapy was the missing link, and this was something I could see myself doing well into my seventies. So, at 48-years-old, I took charge of my life and went back to school to get my master's degree and became a Licensed Mental Health Therapist.

Unfortunately, while in school, my mother passed away. On the day I was to drive my son to college, I received a phone call from my brother, explaining he needed help, some time off from caretaking our mother, who was now 98 years old. We were near the end of her life, and I knew I needed to go. I remember crying on the plane because my heart was breaking in two. I was losing the two people I loved the most in the world: my son, who was launching his new life and my mom, to whom I was about to say goodbye.

Those last few weeks with my mom were terrific, fulfilling, heartbreaking, and humbling. To watch someone in the later stages of dementia is challenging. I have been blessed with a great, albeit, sick sense of humor. At this point, I was aware she might not recognize me. Months earlier, while she was lucid, I made a point to tell her I loved her and how she was a wonderful mother. I said goodbye. Now I was the caretaker, and she referred to me as "that girl." Hearing this was more difficult for my brother than me. She did ask me one day, "Do they know?" Know what Mom? "Just how wonderful you are at your job? I would love to tell your boss how much I appreciate you." Thanks, Mom, I think he already knows (as I looked upward!)

Hospice nurses are angels on earth! I don't know what I would have done without them. They taught me how to take care of her and assist her to die in peace and with dignity. I knew we only had hours to go when the nurse instructed me to "crack her window so the angels can get in to take her home." At that point, I would do anything to help her no longer be in pain. I cracked her window and sat down in the living room for the first time in days. I dozed off only to be awakened by the entire house rattling from a gust of wind, on a windless day. I chuckled to myself, "one angel wasn't enough; you needed an entire brigade!" I went to check on her, and sure enough, she had taken her last breath and was on her final journey. Her celebration of life was full of friends and family who traveled to share our loss and tell our favorite stories of her. So many memories, so much love.

After her death, it took me a bit to get my feet back on the ground. Apparently, while I was away that semester, the school I was attending had a new system, and they were not quite sure how I fit in. After many emails and personal visits with the head of the department, it was sorted out, and I re-entered the program. It took four years, but I was finally able to hang my shingle. For the next three years, I worked at a local drug and alcohol rehab hospital. The grind was rigorous; I worked at the hospital four days a week, 12 hours a day, and in my private practice the other three days. I needed the hours at the hospital to learn clinical skills and acquire my hours for licensure. Besides that, people didn't just run into my office because I put out a sign! I had a leg up going into priva[...] practice because I previously ran my own fitness business ar[...] ceramics business. I had the business acumen, and I cou[...] focus on marketing and learning how to be a better therapi[...] School is only basic knowledge; real learning comes fro[...] being in the field. My skill set was honed and learned fro[...] some of the best in the business. My experiences became [...] valuable asset that would make me a better counselor. I ha[...] LIVED through many of the issues my clients would [...] discussing. My journey had just begun.

Chapter 2

A River Runs Deep:
Friendship

Recently I was invited to an end-of-summer happy hour. It was an evening full of women, some of whom knew each other, and others whom we were meeting for the first time. Our hostess invited us to be in a circle (more on this later) and go around and tell the most exciting thing about our summer. There were stories of travel, marriages, grandbabies, divorce, new jobs, old jobs, new and past loves. What struck me the most, however, is the word "transition." "Transition" was the theme of the evening, and it was used by almost every woman that night. Each of them talked about a past or upcoming transformation or a new phase of life. Women live in continual transition, from little girls, teenagers, adults, single, married, divorced, widowed, empty nesters, to work or not work! No matter the stage each woman presented, she was lifted and given space to tell her story, free from judgment.

We go through many trials and tribulations throughout our lifetime. If we are fortunate, we have great friends who have come along for the ride; our circle is eclectic and broad! Yet, for many, the community may be small or nonexistent. The friend circle at happy hour was symbolic. It represented a group of women whose love and support were never-ending. It was a circle of friendship. It was a circle of welcoming and encouragement. It was a circle of new and well-established friendships.

Clients come to me when they are stuck, sometimes behind a pebble and other times behind a massive boulder. They come to therapy to get out from around the obstacle and back into the flow. Marriage, death, divorce, babies, anxiety, depression, abuse, and substance abuse are some obstacles each of us face. People are fully autonomous individuals who are capable of putting in the effort required to realize their full potential and bring about positive changes in their lives; they are the free-flowing current.

Long gone are the days of sewing circles. Women, often members of one family, would gather around to make quilts. During these sessions, the art of quilt making was passed along to the young girls in the family. More importantly, during these sessions, family stories were told, and values were passed down from generation to generation. Women were supported; they were encouraged to share their experiences. Wisdom, insight, and knowledge spread from the elders to the young girls.

We don't regularly see this today. People are busy. Family of origin rarely live in the same city, let alone on the same side of the country. Women miss the feeling of being part of a community. We see women finding this closeness with friends, networking groups, bible studies, and book clubs. This group acts as the old sewing circle did. Behind every successful woman is a society of women who have her back, her soul, her heart, her best interest in mind at all times. This community supports her dreams, her goals, and her crazy ideas. They go to their events, share their posts, and celebrate their victories. They buy what she's marketing. They push each other out of their comfort zones.

As a therapist, I help people in many areas: divorce, addiction, depression, anxiety, grief, and trauma. My clients include men, women, and couples. Often the reason women come to see me is because of the challenges they are facing. Some of the transitions are very difficult and sorrowful, others cruel. Many times women come to me due to a crisis, and inevitably, we discuss friendships. Women in their thirties, forties, fifties, and sixties are struggling with confidence because of judgment, often during transitions. Every day women hear the opinions of the media, Instagram, Facebook, and Google telling them what to do, what to wear, what size they need to be, whether to be a stay-at-home mom or work. The pressure is enormous. Over the years, this idea has made me curious. The notion of women struggling with friendships at this time of their lives surprised me.

Was friendship something taken for granted? Are there any friendships that survive the test of time? Is it assumed to be more difficult for women in their twenties? Do friendships survive? A 2009 Dutch study found that a vast majority of friendships only last about seven years. Like a relationship, friendships take work if you want them to la To be connected for a lifetime, you must know that you a your best friend won't be the same people as the years go You're not going to have a successful relationship witho speaking up about your needs, desires, and expectations. Y need to talk about issues and forgive each other wh misunderstandings happen. Because as we all kno misunderstanding *will* happen.

It's interesting because most women say we're all for sisterhood, right? But when push comes to shove, wh somebody is doing something great, are we standing beh them, cheering them on, or are we pulling them down? Hav discussed this in networking groups, friend circles, a sessions, I've learned, there are two different types friendships. One is a healthy, positive friend, and the othe women who are tough on other women.

Women, by nature, are intuitive. Women are each othe emotional support system. Girlfriends have a distinctive of reading emotions and intuitively recognizing what need be done, then acting on it. We understand each other; validate each other, we give marriage and breakup advice each other; we share some of our deepest darkest secrets. share the honest truth; we share intimate family details; share beauty products; we tell each other when we have fo in our teeth or when our shirt is on backward, or when we wearing two different earrings. We share lasting memories with each other. When women get together, we gush about our sex lives, our marriages, and details about our significant others and family drama; when guys get together, rarely is any of this discussed. Women rely on each other not only for a shoe-shopping partner but also to share those deep dark secrets, those secrets that not all men may want to hear. There is something beyond exceptional about the female bond that women have with each other.

Recently a woman shared she had received a promotion. When she told her "best friend" of twenty years the news, the friend did not congratulate, share, ask questions, or celebrate. The woman felt rejected and was deeply hurt. She was unable to process why the friend would be so dismissive.

A friend expects her girlfriends to be supportive during the good times, as well as the bad. Women state it is hurtful when they do not feel lifted by their girlfriends. Friends can be empathetic even when they don't agree with someone's opinion or behavior. Women have stated they felt alienated and judged by other women. While women can be so demonstrably good for one another, we also need to work at curbing the dark, destructive tendencies that only knock us down. Women express the biggest shock in these later years is they never imagined struggling with friendships at this point in their lives.

As women, we learn from an early age that we compete with each other. Society values men more, so we vie for their attention and approval to earn a seat at the table. It is crucial to observe feelings when they arise. Fear, jealousy, lack of self-confidence can all be at play. For some, women learned this way of treating other women during the teen years and unfortunately carried it forward into adulthood. Some women assumed high school dramas were how women are and did not move forward. I do not believe females necessarily want to cause harm to one another. Many of us simply don't realize the influence and power we wield. We don't appreciate that our careless whispers or outright nastiness can and does take a harsh toll on self-esteem, confidence, and the ability to thrive and reach full potential in life.

I recently interviewed a client, and she said she did not trust women. She refused to let her husband have conversations with women, even close friends, if she was not around. She refused to let him help neighbors if they were females, especially if they were alone in the house. She convinced herself that "one thing leads to another, and this is how affairs happen." She went on to tell me this had happened several times in their friend circle. The lack of trust was isolating for her and her husband. The husband was the neighborhood fix anything type of person, and he was no longer allowed to help his neighbors, which led to many difficult discussions for them. She was convinced that women were not to be trusted

This person was dealing with past hurts and was missing out on positive relationships, based on history.

The women I know are my biggest support network. They're the first people to celebrate my good news, to come over with wine to commiserate hard times, and they're the loudest voices pushing me to succeed or to tell me "stop it" when I'm getting in my own way. My group has carried each other through new jobs, marriages, miscarriages, and grief.

A million factors go into a lifelong friendship, and no two bonds are alike, but there is one key thing that all ride-or-die friendships have in common – crystal clear communication. Women, from their 20s to 80s, want the freedom to be authentically themselves in their friendships, without fear of being judged. This provides a solid foundation for the friendship to grow, thrive, and become a forever and lasting friendship. You may not agree with all of your friend's life choices, and that's completely okay, but if you want to remain friends with someone for life, you need to accept your friend for who they are and love them for it. Nobody wants to be friends with someone who's just going to judge or criticize them. Keep it judgment-free.

There is still much work to be done. Therefore, I believe in girls 'n giggle nights, women's retreats, networking, and support groups. Women want and need to talk about life's issues, discuss their joys and wounds, learn how to deal with transitions. Women want to inspire and motivate one another to be good friends. Many women did not have good role models. We cannot afford to underestimate the power of female friends; beyond imagination, will you be rewarded.

Long Term Relationships

Long term relationships are beautiful and sometimes rare. To witness or be part of one is inspiring and magical. Some people are naturally great at having long-term friendships. Every garden needs tending; it needs watering, weeds removed, and fertilizer to grow. Friendships require the same commitment. For bonds to grow, they need cultivation. Time, vulnerability, and energy are essential to close relationships, especially in the beginning phase. Every individual and friendship is unique. They can ebb and flow, like a winding river. Some need more attention than others to survive. For some, the passage of time is not a problem. It is possible after not seeing one another for weeks, months, or years to feel an instant connection; it is as if time stood still, nothing has changed. Different relationships might need to be cultivated frequently or risk the chance of them tapering or fading. If a bond is strong, friendships can stand the test of time. If a relationship is essential to you, talk about it, discuss the changes, and how you feel about it.

I am very fortunate. I have friends from when I was 13 years old. All of us are very unique and diverse with where we are with our families, marriages, work, and in the countries we live. We recently reconnected at our 40th high school reunion in Reno, Nevada. We had a fantastic time; it was like time stood still. We realized the following year we would all hit "the big one." (Aren't they all "big" after 30?) Still, we would be turning 60! We decided a celebration was in order. After rounds and rounds of emails and texts, we agreed to meet in Utah to go hiking. One of the ladies, who should be a travel agent, organized the entire trip. She carefully planned out day spas, hikes, outings, and still left us with plenty of downtimes to BE!

These friendships have ebbed and flowed. We have weathered the years when we've lost touch with one another and cherished the times when we have interaction. Our bond was strong; our love was strong; our memories were strong; we survived all the times we missed connecting and continued to support one another no matter what the situation.

It takes one person to suggest an idea. An open invitation was extended to the large friend group. For some, the adventure and timing were perfect, so we began to plan the celebration. It worked out four of us would make the trip to Utah. Once we arrived, we had a fantastic time reconnecting. We spent hours and hours listening to each other. We discussed how we raised our families, the difficulties we faced, the ways we handled it, and who supported us.

Our wonderful travel-agent-girlfriend found us the ideal place to spend our week together near Mount Zion. We rented house, and everyone had a bedroom. It was calm and relaxing There was no TV. There indeed were no cell phones; there wa no Facebook; it was just us. There were activities, but ther was also plenty of downtime. At the end of each day, w reconnected over a great meal and more conversations. Ou days were full, yet it never felt as if we ran from one thing t the next. It was the perfect balance between activity and quie time.

This trip was about self-care, replenishing, connecting, an being vulnerable. It was an opportunity to share in a saf place. We understood, instinctively, there was no judgmen We were not there to compete. We were there to hold spac for each of our stories, and we were eager to learn wha occasions and experiences occurred to create the women w were today. We wanted to get to know who we were a compared to the young, 13-year-old girls we were when w met. (I was the late one to the party; the other three girls me earlier in elementary school.)

To our surprise, all of us had a different view of high school. was interesting to hear new perspectives on the same event Some of the details discovered were new, some old, som scary, many challenging to understand, many sad, and mar were happy revelations. In some ways, it was as if we had nc been present back in high school. At times we were sorry w had not been there for one another. Stressful events shape our lives; we felt sad, not knowing, or being supportive at the time. We realized we missed the happy, joyful events, too. So many situations to shape our thoughts and feelings, yet here we were, still loving and caring for one another as if no time passed.

When you consistently show up and give your friends a safe space, they will let it all out, and you demonstrate to them just how much you care. Sometimes, you don't even need to say anything; you need to listen, be completely present, and be there for them.

Friendships are like any relationship; if they inconsistently pop in and out of your life, you're not going to be happy. When someone only shows up when it's convenient for them, it shows you that they don't value you as much as you appreciate them. It takes more than you alone to keep a friendship going long-term. So, if your friend puts as much effort into the relationship as you do, your connection will stay strong.

Throughout your life, people will come and go. But if you're lucky enough, you'll find a select few individuals who will be there for you long-term. If you want your friends to stay in your life, you need to decide to keep them in your life. Remember to support their dreams, events, and celebrate their victories. Push each other out of your comfort zones.

Clap loudly and cheer for one another! Maintaining a lifelong friendship isn't easy, but it can be done.

Chapter 3

Changing the River Flow:
Enhanced Communication

A colleague came to me recently and said she was good at interviewing people, as therapists are, but she didn't feel she was good at small talk and having just simple conversations. She asked for help to improve her relationships and how to connect more with the people she loves. Women, men, too, tell me one of the things they are looking for is a safe place, a judgment-free zone to connect with others in a more profound, more meaningful way. Sharing thoughts, feelings, and experiences is a vulnerable time and requires grace, empathy, and compassion. Knowing how to begin a conversation is crucial.

Starting with three skills of communication is the most significant way to create intimate connections:

1) Begin sentences with the word "I" rather than "You"
2) No advice-giving
3) Utilize active listening

All of these skills are difficult to do and will require practice to have them feel natural.

One of my favorite roles as a therapist is to lead groups. These groups include cardiac rehabilitation, addiction recovery, women's support, grief/trauma, and business communications groups. A group therapist monitors personalities, behaviors, and must always be acutely aware of the surroundings. When we are in our group, I encourage the clients to start sentences with "I" statements; it's a game-changer. When we communicate with others, we want to do it in the least defensive way possible. Try beginning every sentence with the word "I" instead of "you." The imperial data on this is interesting. When we hear the word "you," we instinctively are reminded of a time when we were children. Often it was accompanied by the index finger. The index finger is often called the "shaming finger."

"You should clean your room." "You should get better grades." "You should listen to me." Sound familiar? As you read the statements, were you able to sense the wagging of the finger? Merely hearing the word "you" takes us back to that place in time when our parents or teachers wanted us to make our bed, save money, study hard, and not talk back to them. They want you to feel and believe that you are wrong, unacceptable, or immoral (or, at best, a disappointment) if you didn't do as they asked.

Although their intentions were in the right place, they often left you feeling "less than." The word "should" indicates that you aren't doing what you would benefit from, and you're not entirely resolute in your choice, either. Should goes hand in hand with self-reproach and is the breeding ground for shame. The problem with shame is that it's worthless, mainly in terms of getting you to do anything. You may have been raised in a house where guilt and shame were used to get you to do all kinds of everyday things, like be helpful to your sister, clean your room and go to church on Sundays. Guilt and shame may feel familiar to you, and humans seek what we know, even if it's terrible. But shame doesn't get you to do the big things like find a job that makes you happy, leave a relationship that sucks the life out of you, or manifest your dreams in love, life and the pursuit of happiness.

There have been studies of both the physical and emotional reactions when someone feels 'shame.' We either cock a hip, or we might take a small step backward with one foot. These are defense positions. We are preparing to secure our viewpoint. The feeling of being shamed is often unknowingly placed on us with words, yet with a new skill set can be avoided. One way to avoid creating a sense of shame is to avoid using the name "you" when we begin a sentence.

Most importantly, though, we stop *listening* because we are busy formulating a defensive response to any question, even if the intent is positive. We want to defend ourselves.

Here is an example:

"You look great today." Sounds like a compliment, right? This statement usually conjures up the response or, at the very least, the feeling of "What? Didn't I look nice yesterday?" Try starting with "I." "I love the shirt you have on today," or "That shirt looks amazing!"

When a sentence starts with anything other than "you," the response is quite different. The person will usually say thank you and continue to talk about the shirt, where they purchased it, how much it cost, and so on. Do your best never to start a conversation with the word "you." It is a challenge! My favorite place to practice? The grocery store! Find things to compliment the clerk without saying *you*! "That smile lights up the store! My favorite line is the speedy one! I feel the energy!" Again, give it a try; it opens an entirely different conversation. Changing the way sentences are started is especially impactful with spouses and children! Due to the lack of judgment, people can receive information without the need to defend their position.

Don't Give Advice/Active Listening

"Hi, do you have a minute? I want you to hear something; need to get it off my chest." After telling the story comes "what you should do, what I would do, you need to..." You shake your head and feel a sense of anger. Your thought is, " don't need you to fix this; did you hear a word I said? I just wanted you to listen." Sound familiar?

> *"The Human Soul doesn't want to be advised or fixed or saved. It simply wants to be witnessed...exactly as it is."*
> *~Parker Palmer~*

Psychotherapy is, at times, misunderstood. One of the stigmas the profession faces is that therapists give advice. Yes, on occasion, this might be true. For most of us, we offer a safe place, a place of freedom to express thoughts and emotions with no judgment. It is a space to reframe old ideas and work through new concepts. Clients are the experts in their lives. They come to realize and to experience this for themselves.

The second part of excellent communication is to avoid advising unless somebody explicitly asks for help. We now live in the age of 'Google,' and answers are retrieved in an instant. People are quick to advise whether it was asked for or not. Thanks, in part to modern technology, we want instant gratification. We have become a society of caregivers and "fixers." In today's society, when we express a thought, the person we are speaking with wants to fix our problem quickly. They want to offer a solution. In my practice, both men and women do this to each other. My prior belief was that men were the culprit, and now it appears very balanced between the sexes. Most people want to vent their thoughts and ideas. They do not want judgments or solutions. They want to be *seen, heard, and validated.*

People *love* to tell you how to live your life. There is no shortage of family, friends, colleagues, neighbors, businesses, and of course, magazines and websites offering plenty of guidance about what you should or shouldn't do. Others want to tell you what or how you should (or shouldn't) eat, drink, shop, vote, believe in (or not believe in), dress, exercise—you name it. But while everyone thinks that telling others what they should do will work, few actually rely on the proven, research-based strategies that actually do result in behavior change.

Why Advice Fails

To be fair, we all find ways to tell others how to live. We can't help it. We all have strong points of view and believe that others should do or think as we do. And most of us are all too comfortable expressing those views to others, whether they're interested or not.

Yet research using reactance theory informs us that whenever a person tells us what to do and how to do it, we respond with defiance because we want to maximize our personal freedom and decision making.

Rarely do friends, family, spouses, or neighbors want advice. As said before, human beings need three things: to be seen, heard, and validated. How many times have you said or heard, "I don't want you to fix it! I want you to listen to me!"? In a nutshell: Advice giving doesn't work, and often completely backfires.

Some of the groups I run are "no advice" zones. It is challenging to do. In today's fast-paced world, technology and lack of social connection, empathy for others is at the lowest point in our history. Giving advice alienates people, it pushes them further away. It does the exact opposite of what most people want: connection and intimacy. Intimacy, in this case, means a close, vulnerable relationship.

Listening is a skill and is seldom taught in today's world. We push people away by telling them what to do. People frequently argue this point. The person giving advice needs to be heard to be in control. The advice-giver feels their position is more important than just listening. When someone is speaking, the advice-giver is rarely using activated listening skills. They are so busy formulating their thoughts that they do not hear what the other person has said. For the most part, people already know what to do; they want and need to vent.

Try following these simple guidelines. If asked for advice, reply by asking if they want help or the chance to vent. If needed, people will say, "yes, I want help." Listen to their story and as close as possible, retell their story back to them: "Is this what I heard?" They will tell you if the story is accurate or insert the missing information. Sometimes, at this point, they will say, "Wow, now I know what to do. Thanks for listening." Job well done, and you didn't need to give any advice! If they insist on help, ask again, "Are you sure you want advice?" I try to ask three times before offering advice. Remember, most of the time, people want to verbalize their thoughts; they don't need answers; they need to be seen, heard, and validated.

When advice is unsolicited and not followed, the beginning of resentments occurs. The next time you are listening to a story, remember - this is the person's chance to vent. Say nothing! Do lots of head nodding and "wow" or "that's interesting." The ONLY time to give advice is after the third attempt of "are you sure you want advice?" This listening skill takes patience and practice. I have witnessed spousal and child relationships blossom when utilizing this skill.

I worked with a gentleman who explained his relationship with his sister as "distanced." It was rare to have a deep, well-connected conversation. He struggled with the skill of listening without advising, as he felt "she needs help." He explained that their strained relationship was years in the making. After weeks of practice in a group environment, he put it to the test. His sister called one day, and he refrained from advising her. He listened and would say, "Wow, that sounds so hard." Or, "What a difficult time it is for you." He explained to me that it was as if a magic door opened, and they talked for hours. He realized she never did need help, just space free of judgment and solutions. She knew what to do all along; she wasn't ready yet. He realized the importance of intentional listening.

Active listening was the third point to examine. It stems from using or hearing the word *you*. Once people hear "you," our minds go into overdrive. We prepare to battle! We are ready to defend our position. Our minds start racing with all the ways to protect ourselves; therefore, we do not listen to what was said to us. If you want to make sure you were heard, add the question, "What did you hear me say?" At first, this will not feel natural and a bit therapeutic; however, it does work. The clue someone is "in their head" and did not hear you is if the person you are talking with cannot repeat back what was said, often saying, "I hear you." Ask, "May I try again?" Usually, this will help the person realize they were not listening.

In my couple's sessions, I have one partner speak then say, "What did you hear me say?" If the partner can repeat (doesn't need to be verbatim), they add, "Is that what you said?" Asking this question allows the first person to either add to their thought, repeat a missing idea, or move forward.

One couple I worked with learned first-hand how very vital this sequence of questions was for them.

One partner stated how they felt on a particular subject and asked, "What did you hear me say?" The second partner repeated back what they heard and asked, "Was that right?" The response was, "Well, mostly. The part that was missing was, *"I love you and want to make our marriage work!"* Wow! The outcome might have been disastrous. Had those words been left out, not heard, could have changed the trajectory of their marriage. Slowing down to make sure each statement is understood is cumbersome, yet valuable. With practice and patience, it will become second nature. Keep trying; the benefits will be worth the effort.

Renew and Restore

Chapter 4

Technology: Friend or Foe?
Time to Start Paddling

My son called from college and said, "Mom, I need help." I froze, as any parent would do when they hear those words. "What's wrong?" He said, "I think I have ADHD." I burst into laughter. He said, "Well, that was the last thing I expected from my mother and a psychotherapist." I said, "You have never had ADHD, and the problem is the thing in your hand." He asked what I meant by that statement. I pointed out he had every notification possible on the phone. "There's a ping, a ding, or vibration for every app on your phone. So yes, you have created Pavlov's dog experiment, and done it effortlessly."

The Pavlovian theory is a learning procedure that involves pairing a stimulus with a conditioned response. Pavlov designed an experiment using a bell as a neutral stimulus. As he gave food to the dogs, he rang the bell. Then, after repeating this procedure, he tried ringing the bell without providing food to the dogs, and he noted that the animals salivated naturally upon hearing the bell.

To be honest, I would be terrible in an office cubicle. With every noise or conversation, my mind would be distracted. Anyone is challenged to stay on task when every 20-30 seconds there is a distraction that says, "You are missing out on something incredible! Look at me!" When, in fact, it has little or no impact on your life now, if ever. The brain is trained, just like Pavlov's dog, to respond to each notification.

Technology is a double-edged sword. It can help with relationships and connections, or it can destroy them. It can improve your social life, or it can turn you into a hermit. For many, it's become a numbing agent: "I can play a game, get on Pinterest, get on Facebook, and I can escape." Zoning out can be a temporary solution to a negative situation, a way to calm down the mind. Yet, for some, it can turn into a more significant problem when overused or not being able to walk away from technology after a few minutes. We have more methods of communication today than ever before, and yet we are more disconnected from each other than any other time in history! Our thumbs are getting a workout, yet our brains are becoming emotionally silent. When is the last time we truly sat down to talk to someone without one eye on a screen? In an era marked by smartphones and electronic gadgets, people have become profoundly disconnected from one another. While we are defined by the communities, workplaces, and relationships that we are part of, are we truly connected to them? Let's face it, we can talk through Bluetooth while driving, but we cannot share facial expressions, a big beautiful smile, or a hug. Emoji faces do not count! I've witnessed co-workers "liking" one another's status updates on Facebook, yet they struggle to enjoy their work together productively. Most everyone I have spoken to feels the impact; however, they struggle to communicate it.

In the past 20 years, the empathy rate has dropped by 40 percent. People are not just escaping work stress; they are also escaping their families, their friends, and loved ones. People are becoming detached and less engaged with what once was important to them.

Empathy comes from hearing intonation, pitch, sound levels, and actual words. Human beings also need to see facial expressions and look into someone's eyes to gather information to acquire emotional intelligence. The human brain knows whether the spoken word is congruent with the facial expression. While our thumbs are getting a workout, our brain is going emotionally silent. It is a way to stay numb to avoid any negative emotional response to a person, place, or thing. When you get on Facebook, Pinterest, or Instagram, they are endless. They were written to be infinite. All of us have surfed on any one of those platforms and endlessly scrolled for minutes or even hours. You start and think, "Oh, I'm just going to look for five or 10 minutes," and before you know it, an hour or two are gone. The application is built to scroll continuously, to never have an endpoint. It is mindless. This time could have been used to spend time with family, make love, go for a walk, read a book, or engage with friends.

Wife: Happy Birthday to you!! Happy Birthday to you!! Happy

Birthday, dead husband!! Happy Birthday to you!!
Husband: Thanks. I assume you meant "dear?"
Wife: Yes!!! That is a crazy autocorrect! Sorry babe.

We use texts to communicate more than ever. Discerning emotion from text is now an essential skill. A new study finds that decoding emails and text is easier said than done, even if it's from a friend. A recent study found that your best friend will find it just as difficult to interpret the emotional tone of your text message as any random person on the street. The research, which is carried out by the <u>Journal of Human Communication Research</u>, demonstrates just how many elements of human interaction we lose in virtual communication. Lost in the transmission is the essential component of social interaction. Text-based communication cuts out many emotional cues we rely on when talking to someone. Body language, such as hand gestures or facial expressions, are vital clues to figuring out what someone means. When we talk to someone, we rely on their tone of voice to transmit emotion. You can try to express your tone of voice using capitals or exclamation points. But HOW WOULD ANYONE KNOW IF YOU'RE ANGRY or you just left caps lock on? And how angry is capitalized ANGRY? It's also almost impossible to figure out if someone is sarcastic or serious.

Technology and I have a love/ hate relationship. I would be upset if my computer, iPad, iPhone, or Kindle were no longer available to me. The benefits of technology are phenomenal and well known. We have the information highway at our fingertips; we can connect to people in an instant; it has changed the way we do business. Adults and children who might be bedridden or need to stay home can connect to the outside world in ways we never knew were possible. It is incredible to watch a momma eagle feeding her young in a nest, see an active volcano, or see someone walk on the moon. Technology is a miracle for all of us in different ways! It can spur imagination and allow people to be creative beyond their dreams. In today's world, we are more connected than ever, and yet we are the most disconnected with one another than any other time in history.

Each generation has faced this same dilemma. My family's first TV was delivered to the house when I was six years old! My mom disliked the TV at first, and she developed rules for the TV. We could watch only during certain hours and watch particular programs. Mom worried our minds would be 'hijacked" or pumped full of "silly ideas." Sounds familiar, right? The point is that it was allowed with boundaries. As our mother, she oversaw what and how we received information. She determined that technology would not replace our outside playtime, and we were not allowed to be watching TV if we had friends or visitors in the house. Mom knew people would always come first! We argued about the rules; she remained firm. She was in charge and was bound to keep us safe.

Does anyone remember the rotary phone? As a teenager, took the kitchen rotary phone handset, stretched it around the corner for a private conversation. The original cord was perhaps 3 feet long, but eventually, with time and use, it could expand twelve feet into the next room! Back then, if someone wanted to reach you, they called back until you answered. We were not tied to these devices as we are today, and we had boundaries. A half-hour of TV a day and seldom on the weekend was allowed; similarly, phone calls were limited to fifteen minutes (unless mom was out of the house or asleep!) Never were we allowed to answer the phone during meals People called back if they wanted to talk; if we were grounded, the TV and telephone were the first things taken away as punishment! To make a genuine connection, we need the sound of a voice, facial expressions, and intonation. We can't get these when we have conversations using our thumbs!

Recently I did an experiment where I wrote "Have a Grea Day!" on the whiteboard. There were nine people in the room and there were nine different versions of what that meant to them – everything from a cheery "Have a great day" wish to a sarcastic, "Oh, have a great day."

It was interesting to have nine versions of one sentence When you read an email or text, the interpretation might be according to your mood; it may not be how the sende intended the message. This disparity, too, is what happen when people rely solely on text or email messages for their primary form of communication. Emoji was added to help with this, and even these are left up to interpretation and may cause confusion for the reader. It is so important to bring back conversations where we sit with people, make eye contact, and have a chance to read their expressions. To make a genuine connection, we need the sound of a voice, facial expressions, and intonation. We cannot get these when we have conversations using our thumbs! When people are in my office, they often speak about "conversations," and it is vital to know if the main instrument was a voice or thumb. The only way we have empathy is if we can read somebody's facial expressions and hear the intonation in their voice, and we can't do that over text messages.

One client came in very distressed over a "conversation" with a girlfriend. She was hurt and angry with what was said. They "talked" for two hours. Then it dawned on me, "How were they talking?" I asked if, by "communication and talking," did she mean voices or texting? Texting. I asked her to read me part of the "conversation." The intonation was full of animosity, frustration, and anger. I asked for permission to read the same thread. Not having an investment in the outcome, I was able to read it straight forward. The emotion poured into her words were feelings SHE placed on the words. Was it possible that was NOT the way her friend intended?

I encouraged her to speak, with words, to her friend to see if there was a possible misunderstanding.

Before Facebook, it was always special to receive birthday wishes on your big day! Today, the thumbs-up, or "like" symbol has become the new way to acknowledge a birthday. If a person is close to you, and you want to stay connected, make their day, pick up the phone to call and wish them a special birthday message. Leave a message if necessary. My friends know by now if you don't pick up the phone on your Birthday, I will sing Happy Birthday to you! It's true; my friends try to pick up rather than listen to me sing!

Texting is fantastic for quick check-ins, updates, and some emojis. If you want to know how someone is, call them! The only way you will know is by the sound of their voice. When we ask people via text, "how are you?" more than likely, we get a one-word reply, "Fine." Do you know that? It is easy for someone to hide their emotions while leaving you clueless about how they are doing. There are a few things we can al do to improve our connection and create boundaries with technology.

First, turn off all notifications! Scary, right? Remember Pavlov's experiment? Trust me, all of us glance at our phones enough throughout the day; missing a text message Instagram, or Facebook notification rarely happens. A nice benefit might be you notice less anxiety while giving your nervous system a chance to calm down.

Second, keep the phone away if you are talking to another human being. Please get in the habit when you are with another person to give them your full attention. And yes, this means store clerks and attendants. They deserve respect as much as the next person. Put your phone away. Stop looking at your wristwatch! Many human interactions are less than five minutes long, and you will survive! It is annoying to be interrupted by vibrations, pings, and dings. It interrupts both the train of thought and the continuity of a conversation.

We all have that person in our lives who have what seems like a permanent extension of their hand. They check their phones regularly. With every notification, the conversation is interrupted. Perhaps it is understandable when someone is on the clock for work; however, phones have invaded personal space and personal time. If you are expected to be on the phone 24/7 for work, that is an entirely different issue. Most people make it a bad habit. Most importantly, it tells the person, "I have more important people or things to do than talk with you!"

There was a recent study to see what happens if a phone is in someone's hand or on the table. The study wanted to see if the person was approachable. When a person had a phone in their hand or on the desk, people were less likely to say hello or stop for a quick conversation. When there was no phone in sight, a boss, a friend, or neighbor was far more approachable.

Third, take a tech time-out at least once a week. Turn off all technology and let the fun begin. Play board games, go for a hike, take a nap, daydream, have sex in the afternoon, read to your kids, bake cookies. See how many creative things you can do when you realize technology is not defining your time. I have my clients create a "boredom jar." They choose a bowl or jar and fill it with all the things they want to do but "forget" when they are bored. Many of the items don't cost a dime: hike a trail, bike, sit by the ocean, coupon, journal, play the guitar, learn a new language, to name a few. Try it; it is fun!

Out of my concern for the lack of connection with others, I recently kicked off a grassroots program called Cultivating Community. The mission statement is "to provide meaningful conversation which leads to positive change." We meet monthly at a local restaurant (a win-win for both of us). The idea is we learn to put away our technology for one hour! I admit this is difficult. At various times we want to share photos, look up information, or explain an idea. It is laughable how fast we grab our phones rather than discuss an idea. The benefits have been fantastic. People are learning to communicate with their neighbors, networking happens, and we are mindful! Pulling out phones is a distraction; ideas, thoughts, observations vanish in an instant. The choice is ours to make. We can pledge to improve our community by lifting one another, to increase and stimulate all that is wonderful and unique around us. We can make changes, both large and small, to connect with one another. The next time you are with someone, try saying, "We have such little time together; let's not use any tech devices and be mindful while we are together."

Process Addiction

In the office, I see more and more what we call "process addictions." A process addiction is compulsive. The compulsion to continually engage in an activity or behavior despite the negative impact on the person's ability to remain mentally and or physically healthy and functional in the home and community defines the process or behavioral addiction. The person may find the behavior rewarding psychologically or get a "high" while engaged in the activity but may later feel guilt, remorse, or even overwhelmed by the consequences of that continued choice.

Unfortunately, as is typical for all who struggle with addiction, people living with behavioral addictions are unable to stop engaging in the behavior for any length of time without treatment and intervention.

I have treated children and adults who are on their phones, iPads, Netflix, or social media from 10 to 17 hours a day. Children may not go out with their friends or even avoid getting their driver's license. They delay getting their driver's licenses because they have 200 virtual friends. FOMO: the Fear Of Missing Out is a genuine issue for these children. Some adults are engaging in pornography, online gaming, or shopping as a means to numb emotional pain. When a person no longer manages their life or functions, it is called an addiction. Some of the signs that life is unmanageable are dinner engagements that are ignored or missed; credit cards are maxed out, there is no time for play, no time for family, insomnia due to playing all night, and weight loss or gain. These are all warning signs.

I sit with clients every day and see first-hand how invasive these devices are with people's lives. Go to any restaurant to witness families, all with their devices, tune out one another. Whether it's video games, shopping online, playing a game, or responding to emails, they are ignoring the most important people who are with them. Using technology in this way is destructive and further isolates each member from one another. Every day more and more clients come into my office abusing different types of technology. I see spouses disregard their partner arriving home after work, children isolating in their rooms, no one is getting to know each other, and there is little daily interaction.

Some believe this might be the best-educated generation in history. Still, critics also note shorter attention spans, need for frequent (positive) feedback, lack of independence, poor in-person communication skills, and increased screen time affect our children. Recent studies also indicate that the rate of near sightedness in children under ten has skyrocketed due to phones and iPads. In China, over 75% of kids are nearsighted now! It is not all doom and gloom. Positive suggestions will help young people and adults find balance.

"We cannot change what we are not aware of, and once we are aware, we cannot help but change." (Sheryl Sandberg)

Doesn't it seem like technology happened quickly? It is both scary and exciting to see what is coming next. Every generation has had to deal with the latest form of science. And like every generation before us, it is a matter of placing boundaries. Here are some ways to be a part of positive change to better connection:

The American Academy of Pediatrics recommends:

- For children younger than 18 months, avoid the use of screen media other than video-chatting.
- For children ages 2 to 5 years, limit screen use to 1 hour per day of high-quality programs.
- Be willing to put time limits on games
- Have tech-free zones. Do not allow phones at the dining table or the bedroom.
- Be a good role model. Put your phone away at your child's game, don't text and drive, don't selfie every moment - etch the memory into your brain.
- Turn off all notifications on your phone.
- Encourage verbal conversations rather than text messages.

- Make time for dinner or gather at the end of every day Remember, it is about the quality of time. If dinner is impossible, come together at the end of the day for ice cream or popcorn.
- Check-in and see how everyone is doing by using our voices.

Start observing how much time on technology occurs throughout the day. The first step is to become aware, to notice. Check-in verbally to see how everyone is doing Remember, studies show that the more a family has quality time together, there is less depression, anxiety, and eating disorders.

Over the last few years, technology has advanced at immense speed and has had a significant impact. Some people refer to it as a disaster, while some refer to it as a blessing. There is no doubt that we live in an age where it has become an essential part of our life, but it can sometimes act as a hindrance, too if dependency continues to increase. If we take an overview of the technology, it has made various positive changes in almost every field, whether it's medical, business, education or sports. As human beings, we have the choice to place healthy boundaries with technology and use it positively. It is up to us to focus on human connection, to understand the importance of social interaction, and how vital it is for healthy relationships.

Chapter 5

Whirlpools of Life:
Shame

*You should make your bed. You should get better grades.
You should go to college. You should...*

According to Brené Brown, "*Shame is the intensely painful feeling or experience of believing that we are flawed and therefore unworthy of love and belonging.*"

Along with Brené, I am on a mission to discuss and understand the origins of shame, as well as teach skills to help eliminate the unknowingly harmful effects of using the word "should."

Unresolved shame can lead to feelings of depression, anxiety, and low self-esteem. *Shame* may also be a symptom of some mental health diagnoses, such as body dysmorphia, or the product of a traumatic experience, such as rape or sexual assault.

The word *should* often creates a sense of shame when we hear it because it is a word of judgment, and every time we use the word *should*, we are judging ourselves or judging others. *Should* is an invented concept that is engaged to cause us to feel shame. When people say you "should" do something and you don't, or that you "shouldn't" and you do, they mean—intentionally or unintentionally—to shame you into acting the way they want you to behave. Often these rules were created by parents, grandparents, teachers, society, religion, all who were very well-meaning at the time.

Remember that should's and should not's are random principles agreed upon by the few or the many to encourage conformity. When parents insist that you "must" or "should" make your bed, save money, study hard, or be polite, they want you to feel and believe that you are misbehaving when you do not follow their wishes. The intent may be from the right place, wanting the best outcome for a situation; however, it encourages some people to feel ashamed. And for some, this leads to the feeling of being bad, unacceptable, immoral or, a disappointment if you don't conform. These feelings may lead to a lifetime of feeling unworthy or unlovable. It does not allow the opportunity to think for yourself, to feel better about yourself; you will do as they say.

We place a certain amount of pressure on ourselves with the word *should*. *Should* sets unrealistic expectations, induces guilt, and decreases a desire to do what you want to do. When we use the word *should*, we are not accepting the current situation. When you think about what *should* be, you ignore how it is. For instance, if you think "I should meditate more," it follows that you don't do enough and perhaps are "bad" for not doing more. When we tell ourselves we *should* be doing something, we reinforce the idea that we are not doing it already. Instead of focusing on goals, you begin to worry about the future: "I should do this." *Should* also takes away your autonomy. When you don't accomplish what you set out to accomplish, you end up feeling like you don't have control of your actions. *Should* takes away self-love as it focuses on what you could be like rather than what you are. The word is used to express advice, obligation, or duty; thus, it creates a sense of judgment and disapproval.

The word and its meaning aren't just about yourself. It is about others. You often worry about what others *should* be doing. This type of thinking puts a strain on relationships. When relationships center on expectations, they tend to suffer. *Should* puts pressure on your relationship and leads to negativity; it ignores your accomplishments. Instead of focusing on completed tasks, you overthink how it *should, or might* have been. *Should* doesn't let you focus on the present or celebrate it; rather, it sparks negative emotions. When was the last time you used the word? Do you remember how it made you feel? Unhappy, guilty? If you are thinking about what you 'should' have done, you are unhappy about not having met your future self's expectations. If you think about what you 'should' be doing right now, you are feeling guilty about not doing what is expected of you. And when you worry about what others 'should' be doing, you end up being resentful. So, "*should*" rarely evokes a positive response.

An Exercise: Should

The following is a two-part exercise that was created while working at a substance abuse hospital. Take a piece of paper with the heading "I Should" at the top of the paper. In bullet form, write your "should list."

I should...

- I should not be an addict
- I should love my mother more
- I should be a better dad
- I should live in a different place
- I should own a home
- I should be happy
- I should do volunteer work
- I should lose 10 pounds
- I should quit smoking
- I should be a better parent
- I should be a better wife

Write whatever is your "should" list. Take several days to form this list, and remember, nothing is too big or too small. Keep the list with you and write them down throughout the day. Notice how many times you say "should." This awareness might be eye-opening. The should list just created is YOUR shame list! That is right; the word *should* and shame go hand in hand. It is often deep-seated from childhood. Remember, we cannot change what we do not recognize.

This exercise came from an experience I had working with a man who owned a fortune 500 company. He was in this particular drug/alcohol rehab center for the fourth time and in my men's group for the first time. The group was given this assignment of creating their "should" list. He gathered his list and brought it to me to present in a group session. We decided to put his *should* list up on the whiteboard; he had about 16 or 17 items. He had been in my group for some time; his history was well known to all of us in the group. He built his business from the ground floor, and his individual wealth was numbers many of us could only imagine. His stay at the hospital was his 10th attempt to be sober. The stakes were high; if he relapsed again, he would lose his family and business. A Recovery Contract (a document often used to help define repercussions in case of relapse) was written and signed by all necessary members of the family and business partners. The third thing on his 'should' list was, "I should go back and finish college." That was interesting to me because this man owned a major, major company and was worth billions. Now my curiosity was peaked.

I decided to devise the second phase of this exercise. Take a new piece of paper and at the top of the page, write

If I really wanted to, I could...

At this time, grab your *should* list:
- I should not be an addict
- I should love my mother more
- I should be a better dad
- I should live in a different place

- I should own a home
- I should be happy
- I should do volunteer work
- I should lose 10 pounds
- I should quit smoking
- I should be a better parent
- I should be a better wife

The next question has two parts; both are necessary to answer.

Example:

If I really wanted to, I could...
Own a home.
Question one: Do you really want to own a home? Answer yes or no. YES!

Question two: Can you own a home? NO!

IF THERE IS A "NO" TO EITHER QUESTION, ELIMINATE IT FROM YOUR *SHOULD* list. REMOVE IT FROM YOUR **SHAME** LIST!

Any item with a "no" is something keeping you locked in shame. Shame creates negativity and guilt. More importantly, it keeps you locked in the cycle of feeling worthless, unlovable, and ashamed. Scratch it off your list. Let's read that again:

SCRATCH IT OFF YOUR LIST!

Move any item with two "yes" answers to a goal sheet. (more on this in a moment.)

This person might feel worthless because they do not own a home. It is also possible they are living with parents or renting while saving money for a down payment. There is no shame in saving money! Yet shame keeps us small, resentful, and afraid. Using old thinking patterns keeps people stuck in negative thought patterns.

Here is the rest of the story with the man in the group:

On the board I wrote, "If I really wanted to, I could...." We started a conversation, and I said, "*Can* you go back to college?" Everybody laughed, including him, and he said with a smile, "Actually, I could probably buy a college, or I could build my own college." We all had a good chuckle. I then said, "Do you REALLY WANT to go back to college?" He looked at me; his eyes had welled up with tears. "No," he replied and looked at his shoes. As he looked down, his entire body transformed into a fetal position in the chair, which was challenging to watch; our eyes wanted to divert away from him. His shame was palpable.

The room's silence was broken only by his tearful sobs. We could feel his sense of loss, guilt, and self-hatred. As he lowered his head, I asked him what it was about going back to college. He said, "It was always my father's dream, and I let him down."

An *AHA* moment!

This man was in his forties and owned a billion-dollar company. He keeps the idea of going to college on his "should" list, which has kept him in shame and guilt, even after his father had passed away. Once we processed it, he realized his father was proud of him for his accomplishments. He erased that from the list, then sobbed. For so many years, this "should" weighed heavily on him and contributed to his addictive behavior. This *AHA* moment for him was pivotal in releasing his shame about not going to graduate school, his father, and his sense of worth. Shame loses its hold on us when we *expose it, talk about it, and bring it to light.* We destroy shame once we are willing to be vulnerable and bring it forward for examination.

If things stay on the *should* list, they then move over to a "goal list." Switching it over to a goal list, use the SMART acronym: Specific, Measurable, Attainable, Realistic, and Time-bound.

Now get out a new piece of paper. Write down the acronym, SMART, down the side of the page. Take each item on the "should" list and see if it passes the test.

Example: *I should exercise.*

Specific? No! To be precise, list the type of exercise to be done:

I will <u>ride my bike</u>, or I will <u>lift weights</u>.

These are *specific* forms of exercise.

Measurable? No! List the ways it will be measurable:

> I will ride my bike for <u>twenty minutes</u>, <u>four days a week</u>, or
> I will lift weights <u>three times a week.</u>

It is now *measurable.*

Attainable? Yes! (only you know this answer!)

Realistic? Yes! If it said, "every day," you might need to change the answer due to weather conditions, illnesses, etc. Three or four times a week is more *realistic.*

Time-bound? No! I encourage people to think in small periods; they can adjust accordingly. <u>Six weeks</u> is an excellent amount of time to both set a goal and adjust as necessary.

The new goal would read:

> I will ride <u>my bike</u> for <u>twenty minutes</u>, <u>four days a week</u>, for the next <u>six weeks.</u> It is specific, measurable, attainable, realistic, and timebound.

Once a "should" is turned into a goal, erase it from the "should" list. This exercise frees people up from the guilt and shame that comes with the word *Should*.

Change A Word, Change A Conversation.

"Why would you do it that way?" "Um, well, um, well" Instant judgment. The person asking the question doesn't mean to create defensiveness, yet "why" questions create us to cringe and wonder what we did wrong. It creates a negative thinking pattern. The difference between a 'what' and a 'why' question is the implication of judgment and lack of curiosity. When asking 'why' questions, we can instantly feel judged. Asking 'why' is often a way of communicating disbelief, implying that it's the wrong decision. If I asked someone, "Why are you wearing that shirt today?" The likely response is, "Well, um, don't know. I kind of liked it." You'll stutter, you get defensive about why you're wearing that shirt. By changing from a 'why' question to a question of curiosity, "What made you wear that shirt today?" more than likely the answer would be, "Oh, you know, I just got it out of the laundry" or "I just went to Stein Mart and thought the colors were hot. It goes with my shorts."

The person will tell a story. Uncovered are many more details and information. It creates curiosity. Consider: "What brought you here today? Or What brings you in today?" versus "Why are you here?" The first two questions are open-ended and will illicit information. The third question might cause me to feel shame or the need to defend myself, and it creates a massive opportunity for shutting down.

Sometimes these negative thinking patterns emerge from childhood and continue into adulthood. I can remember some of my "why" questions - "Why did you get a C in math? Why did you make the bed that way? Why did you hit your brother?

Why are you acting that way? Why would you do that? Why are you crying?" It can be argued that the question 'why?' is hardwired into our psyche. It becomes almost instinctual to ask 'why' when we want more information or to discover the motives behind actions — in reality, asking 'why' is a habit. It's easy, and one of the reasons young children use it (can you remember the terrible 2's: why?, why?, why? Ahhhh!!!) They may not have acquired the language to paraphrase. What they mean is, 'I don't understand, please explain.' Asking 'why' is often a way of communicating disbelief, implying that it's the wrong decision. With our more sophisticated grasp of communication, we don't need to rely on 'why.'

The Whodunnit List

Most of us are looking for solutions to problems, just like the little child. "Why" questions, since they feel like judgment, shut down the thinking, investigative process. The goal is to open and gain new insights. Asking open-ended questions appeals to our sense of curiosity in a non-threatening way. Try using the whodunnit list of "who," "what," "when," "where," and "how."

So instead of "why" you might ask:

- "What is it that attracts you to this option at this time?"
- "How did you arrive at this decision?"
- "Might you get further information?"
- "Who else might you ask?"

- "What tells you that now is a good time to make this change?"
- "What other options have you explored?"
- "Can you tell me more about that?"

All of these questions open up the issue in a way that "why" never will. By substituting "why" with the other open questions, you help draw out a person's inner resources. "Why" may be quick, but the other open questions, especially "how" promote action. "Why" may often trigger a stress response which puts us into a state of survival (the classic fight, flight, or freeze response) where we are only able to access a limited range of cognitive responses. "How come?" is a more relaxed approach, which is more likely to enable us to evoke a broader range of cognitive and emotional responses on which we can build. Just try to use "why" sparingly and get in a better habit of asking open-ended questions to gather and cultivate more profound, more intimate conversations.

A young boy, full of excited smiles, walked into the house with his report card to show his mom. Brimming with delight, he handed it to her. "Why did you get a C in math?"

His smiles turn to tears of sadness when he realizes his mother is disappointed. In a split second, he feels shame, defeated; he hurts because she is displeased.

Ultimately, all of us want a safe place to land. As a parent, spouse, or co-worker, we want to create a space for others to express themselves without the worry of retribution. By changing one word, connection, safety, understanding, and vulnerability have a secure space to land.

Let's look at the same situation with a different outcome:

"Before I look at your card, tell me how you feel about it." "Look, mom! I got a C in math!" Mom notices he is all smiles, "tell me more about it." "Two weeks ago, I forgot to hand in my homework, so it was an F! I worked really hard, did some extra credit, and I got it to a C! Isn't that cool?"

By allowing this child to tell his story, to express the pride in what he accomplished, he feels like a winner. There is plenty of time to figure out what was going on two weeks ago. Yet, the child before you is so proud of themselves, the moment ought to be celebrated! If a safe place is created, and the other person knows it is consistent, they will open up more and more to you! The safe space, complete with curiosity, allows people the freedom to tell the truth. When they are not so busy protecting their position, they'll tell a story, often elaborating on the details, which is probably far more significant than the actual situation that happened.

This same connection can occur in a business setting:

"Why is the report late? You have been messing up lately."

This person, more than likely, will respond defensively.

By making simple adjustments, the questions provide a safe space for gathering more information.

"I'm concerned about the department. It seems things are a bit off; can I hear more about the report being late?"

"Yes, last week, my mom was placed in hospice. It's been really rough."

Changing "why" questions to "whodunnit" questions provide space to be vulnerable, to state our truth, to gather information. And while it may be difficult to break this seemingly innocent and well-intentioned habit, start slow by being aware of language, and be willing to make small, simple changes. In doing so, a world where defensiveness and worthlessness live will instead become the birthplace of joy, connection, belonging, vulnerability, and empathy.

Chapter 6

On the River Bank:
Boundaries

While growing up, there was always a reason to be in or around the Truckee River. I have fabulous memories of fishing, rafting, and swimming in the freezing water that ran from Tahoe City to Pyramid lake. The river is a source of recreation, research, and wildlife with festivals and leprechauns (it was turned green on St. Patrick's Day) utilizing the beauty and strength of this fantastic river. Today its banks remind me of boundaries, the same way a bank is used to contain the river while it moves downstream. Boundaries keep us safe, as well as secure, while we navigate this journey. The water represents us moving through life; sometimes, it moves swiftly while clearing a path for the river to move forward, and other times the water, like life, meanders along. The creation of the bank was subtle, took place over a long period of time, just like Codependency. According to the Mental Health America website, Codependency is "a learned behavior that can be passed down from one generation to another. It is an emotional and behavioral condition that affects an individual's ability to have a healthy, mutually satisfying relationship."

Once I delved into being a therapist at both the addiction hospital and private practice, it was time to embrace my belief in healing the mind, body, and spirit. As I have mentioned, self-examination is part of the territory. This part of my story required me to look at the codependence and boundary setting.

The first step was to read the book, *Codependent No More*, by Melody Beattie. Several professors and colleagues suggested reading this book to help my clients. As I settled in on a rainy day to read the book, highlighter in hand, I soon discovered this book was for *me!* I switched highlighters and read the book with earnest and curiosity about this dysfunction called Codependency. Seeing personal behaviors written in a book felt like being in a kayak with no paddle - scary, out of control, revealing. It would take introspection, self-compassion, and willingness to find both paddles and steer my own kayak. In the years ahead, there would be times when the current was so swift it felt like I was going backward; there were other times the water was so low the kayak needed to be picked up and carried downstream. The journey has been worth the effort; boundaries are placed to protect us, keep us emotionally and physically safe, like a riverbank, containing us from the discomfort if the water overruns the bank. As I tell my clients, let's learn to *"be comfortable with feeling uncomfortable!"*

During this time of self-introspection, I reflected on some of the character traits that held me captive since my childhood. I had low self-esteem, looking to anyone or anything for a boost of confidence and approval. I worked to make everyone happy and avoided confrontation.

I had little understanding of my own needs or likes and thrived from "helping others," which just served as a lousy cover-up for attempting to control or manipulate one into needing me. Codependent behaviors are adaptive (positive) coping skills we learn as children. When not refined, they become maladaptive (negative) behaviors as an adult. An excellent example of this is the use of a pacifier for a baby. We use pacifiers (or thumbs) to help babies learn how to self-soothe themselves. If a child is never taught other healthy means to self-soothe (meditation, distraction, thought stopping), they may later turn to drugs or alcohol for the same self- soothing effect, yet these methods are maladaptive.

Boundaries help to remedy and liberate a codependent. A limit brings forth the opportunity to truly love and care for another individual in a healthy fashion while encouraging self-ownership (of the good and bad). Simply put, boundaries allow us to learn self-control and independence by handling our own problems. When we begin to practice boundary setting, we begin to understand we can no longer control or manipulate others, love or act out of feelings of guilt or obligation, or take on the resentment building responsibilities that aren't ours to take on in the first place. We also begin the problematic, humbling process of respecting others' boundaries and limitations.

At the root of many codependent behaviors is the notion ' don't deserve, or I'm not good enough." A shift occurs while learning to place boundaries. A sense of empowermen transpires; it allows people to "like" themselves, permit them *to **be.***

Some codependent characteristics include (via the MH/ website):

- An exaggerated sense of responsibility for the action of others
- A tendency to confuse love and pity, loving people the can rescue
- A tendency to do more than their share
- A tendency to become hurt when others don' recognize their efforts
- Holds onto a relationship to avoid feelings o abandonment
- An extreme need for approval and recognition
- A sense of guilt when asserting themselves
- Lack of trust in others, and the need to control others
- Difficulty making decisions

There is tremendous power in the words we choose. When we speak a thought or put it in a sentence, we are putting it ou in the universe. At some point, the words we use will come back to us as an experience. Don Miguel Ruiz's book ,"The Four Agreements," is a major tenet in my life. The firs agreement is, "Be Impeccable with Your Word. Speak with integrity. Say what you mean. Avoid using the word to speak against yourself or to gossip about others. Use the power of your word in the direction of truth and love."

Once the shift to this principle occurred, the partial understanding of why my boundaries were weak or nonexistent became more evident. Up to this point, I had not selected or taken my words sincerely; my words were not impeccable. By uttering statements such as "I'm so stupid I forgot the milk," or "What an idiot, why'd I do that?" left me feeling "less than," miserable. Did I truly believe I was stupid or an idiot? Were these words *impeccable?* I had let myself down, time and time again, by going back on my word. Words are the foundations of our lives, even when they are subconscious. Once the shift occurred, I learned to catch my negative self-messages and thinking patterns. Learn to catch undesirable or to limit words and change them!

The times when I went back to an ex-boyfriend, agreed to take on more work than I could handle, said yes when I wanted to say no, were times when I didn't like myself. And in a way, breaking this boundary made it easier to continue seeing myself as not good enough, smart enough, pretty enough, worthy enough. Breaking a boundary made it somewhat OK to be down on me.

How do you shift from not being okay to being okay with who

you are? Step one is to learn how to be less judgmental o
yourself. Learn to have compassion and give yourself grace
let yourself be, appreciate both the good and bad about you
Maybe you raise your voice at someone out of frustration
Afterward, you may say things like, "Why did I just do that?"
"Why am I such a bad friend?" or "I'm so stupid for saying
what I did." But instead of judging yourself in that way, wha
if you felt the feeling the action brought up and accept tha
you regret what you said? Self-compassion, I've learned, is ar
option.

What that means is allowing yourself to experience whateve
it is that you are feeling without judging that feeling: to see
yourself apart from the emotions so that you can observe
without evaluation, but with understanding. The more you
accept yourself as you are, the more you take yourself wholly
the easier it is to place healthy boundaries. Compassion anc
empathy replace negativity, self-loathing, and judgment.

Healthy boundaries come in different forms, both personally
and professionally. My word being impeccable is one
boundary; another is the boundary of time. Therapists ofter
have 50-minute sessions. By consistently starting on time, as
well as ending on time, I respect both my time and my client's
time by role modeling the healthy behavior. By doing this, i
sets others' expectations and keeps my boundaries. Both
emails and text messages have boundary dilemmas. How
quickly does one have to respond?

One client came in and said, "I emailed everyone yesterday (Sunday), and one member of my staff replied! What's wrong with them?"

We discussed the boundary predicament. If the staff member sees their boss sending emails on Sunday, in the middle of the night, or at 6 am, the employee might feel required to respond (especially if the team member doesn't have healthy boundaries). The employee might worry that the boss will see them less favorably when it comes to promotions or raises. We discussed expectations and setting boundaries with her staff.

If more time is necessary to figure something out, learn to say, "I don't know the answer right now; I'll have to get back to you on that." Learning to say no to someone can be difficult for some people. Learn to validate the person, "I appreciate you considering me. Right now, it is not a good time for me." Saying no becomes empowering when you no longer do things you didn't want to do in the first place. The more you start paying attention to what you want and need, the more you will strive to take care of yourself.

It's more than likely that at some point, you will break a boundary; the key is not to get upset with yourself after the fact. Again, it comes back to being able to see yourself without judgment. If you go back on your word, recognize that you've done so, and try to understand what led to you doing so. Then

after you know it, let yourself off the hook and go back to th
beginning.

Has a loved one ever asked you for a significant favor o
commitment, something you dreaded, but you agreed to do i
to avoid hurting their feelings? Or, maybe you worried that i
you said "no," they wouldn't love you as much? Many of u
have done this from time to time. But do you also remembe
how you behaved as a result of this undesired favor o
commitment? Were you loving and generous, remindin,
yourself that the other person had probably done many kin
things for you over the years? Or, were you instead resentfu
toward them, half-hearted or just plain old grumpy regardin,
the activity, wishing the whole thing would be over with a
quickly as possible?

That's the difficulty with ignored boundaries. When yo
ignore your own or set limits that are too loose for you
comfort zone, you end up engaging in activities that com
with a built-in negative perception. This isn't to say you shoul
never help a partner, family member, or friend. But if yo
regularly say "yes" to things you don't want in your life, hov
much are you helping them? How much are you helpin,
yourself?

Types of Boundaries

Boundaries work in two directions: they permit or prohibi
others from getting closer to you, and they determine hov

close you can get to someone else. The above scenario represents just one type of boundary. Boundaries fall into four basic categories: **physical** (personal space), **cognitive or thought** (belief systems, opinions), **emotional** (including expression of feelings, lack of emotion or lack of control) and **spiritual** (not related to religion but to what feels right and life-supporting to you).

If you set overly rigid boundaries, you shut people out, whether it's your intention. When you fail to set boundaries, or when they're too loosely defined, you send others an inadvertent message that you're ready and willing to be taken advantage of, only to turn around and resent the other person for doing precisely what you permitted them to do.

According to noted psychotherapist Mary Sanger of Insights Collaborative Therapy Group in Dallas, "It's your job to determine how closely you let others in, and also your job to contain yourself so that you don't intrude on someone else's boundaries." The tricky part is that boundaries are different for everyone. For example, while one person may be very comfortable with hugs from a stranger, someone else may recoil at the very thought. So, something as "simple" as hugging someone whom you already know doesn't like being hugged is intruding on his or her boundary. Saying "yes" to a friend when you know you should say "no" is trespassing on your own boundary. And no matter how you rationalize away your behavior, neither of these scenarios show respect for the

the other person's thoughts or feelings, or your own.

Boundary Setting 101

If raised in a home where boundaries were not identified and respected, you might still find yourself, as an adult, struggling with them. Perhaps you were even taught that it's selfish to say "no" or that "no" required a lengthy explanation attached to it. To learn to set boundaries, you're going to need some new tools in your toolbox.

Believing that your needs, preferences, and opinions are just as crucial as everyone else's is the first step is boundary setting. Make a list of:

- Five things you enjoy doing
- Five things you *don't* enjoy doing
- Five values that are highly important to you (e.g., family, friends, career, free time, physical activity, nature, etc.)
- Five types of behavior that you will not tolerate in yourself or others.

You now have a good starting point for how and where to set boundaries that are meaningful to you. For example, if you love spending time with family but get very annoyed when family members arrive late to planned activities, there's a boundary you can set. You may not be able to control their punctuality, but you can communicate to them in a firm but polite way how you feel about it and ask them to cooperate.

Look around you. Is there a friend, teacher, clergy member, or someone else whose boundary style you admire? How do they listen to others? How do they honor themselves when doing so? How do they decline an undesired request made of them? How do they handle rejection? Make mental notes of what you like (or don't) in others' boundary setting so that you can model your behavior after theirs during the learning process.

Are Boundaries Firm, or Flexible?

The answer is, both. When you first try out new boundaries, this may be especially challenging. Boundaries are sort of like a new pair of leather shoes; you need to "break them in" before they're comfortable. And limitations, like good shoes, also require that you take good care of them, never neglecting them. The good news is, with practice, regularly used boundaries will serve you well for a lifetime; you no longer need to take things personally or worry so much about other people's feelings or opinions. You are responsible for yours, and they are accountable for theirs. When healthy boundaries are in place, they do much of the work for you.

Handling Boundary Missteps

It *will* happen; either you'll step over someone else's boundary, or they'll step over yours. But as you practice honoring your own and others' boundaries, you'll begin to see missteps for what they are: mistakes or blunders that can be owned and or corrected. Not everyone will embrace your limitations, and you may not understand someone else's; both things are OK. Sometimes boundary missteps are even intentional. Addressing them as they occur helps prevent feelings from building up inside you.

One of the ways to handle boundary slips is using the "I feel" exercise. For example, "*I feel* unimportant when you are late for our dates. I'm asking that you either be on time or at least let me know when to expect you." Being honest about your feelings and communicating them to others are essential components of the boundary setting process. If you're unsure of whether a boundary has been crossed, check in with your feelings. If you feel angry or resentful, it's a pretty good sign that you need to speak up.

Try looking at boundaries not as rigid walls but as fences— with gates. You can decide what does (and doesn't) get past that gate. Yes, we use gates to protect ourselves, but we also use them to invite others in when we're ready. In that scenario, we can genuinely and authentically enjoy their company.

Rowing a kayak is another excellent way to assess behaviors and feelings. You are not alone in the kayak; therefore, you are not solely responsible for rowing; in fact, every now and then, STOP rowing the kayak to make sure that the others in the kayak are right there with you, rowing along and doing their share. You do not need to tell anyone how to row or help them see that they are not rowing (that's their own business). And, you do not need to maintain relationships where the other people in the kayak aren't rowing.

Healthy boundaries are safe and empowering. If feelings of frustration or resentment arise, maybe it means you need to do more work on caring for yourself. Perhaps it means you need to be more assertive, but know that setting boundaries is a daily practice, and maintaining them is all about where you fall on the spectrum of self-esteem.

Your True North

When clients state, "I don't know who I am," or, "I don't have any close friends," it raises my sense of curiosity about their situation. Do you find yourself always trying to please other people and seek their approval? Are you the 'go-to' person for everyone else's problems? Or maybe you're afraid of being alone or abandoned, so you put up with unhealthy relationships to avoid it? Do you ignore your needs and take care of others? Do you jump into other people's problems? Do you correct something when a spouse or child makes a mistake? All these things are symptoms of Codependency; it is a loss of self because you're too busy taking care of others. Codependency means you over-function in someone else's life and under-function in your life. Over-functioning in someone else's life limits the other person's growth, keeping them from being capable and responsible. Though its intent

may be to help, this type of over-involvement ultimately hurt.
the healthy development of the other person.

Listed below are some of the ways we may be over
functioning in someone else's life when we carry these
behaviors too far:

- Giving: giving gifts beyond your means to feel good o
  impress someone
- Fixing: always finding a solution for someone instead o
  letting them figure it out themselves
- Caretaking: taking care of others when they can do i
  themselves
- Helping: you feel the need to step in and help others
  "Oh, but you are the BEST room mother, we can't do i
  without you." Or, "The ONLY person for the job is you!"
- Thinking for others: "what she means..." Or, "they wil
  do it."
- Speaking for others: "what they meant to say ...."
- Taking over: feeling the loss of control you take ovei
  every situation in your private and work-life
- Controlling: the need to be in control at all times.
- Doing for others what they need to do for themselves.

If you are saying "that might be me," contact a professiona
therapist. Codependency has many nuances, and it is essentia
to have guidance. Codependent behaviors were excellent
coping skills as children; when not replaced with healthy adult
coping skills, they may become maladaptive and cause self-

neglect. What's important to remember, though, is that you're a human BEING, not a human DOING--and you can't do everything for everyone.

The world needs giving, loving, compassionate, and empathic people like you. However, you also need to receive love, kindness, and compassion in return. The concept of the cycle of receiving and giving is sometimes tricky for people who are codependents because they're often in one-sided relationships. However, you're disabling yourself from your authentic path and purpose when you continue to enable others this way. Despite your best intentions, you're also depriving the person you're sheltering of the lessons they need to learn and grow. The truth is, you can only give so much for so long before you start suffering and need help yourself. Your 'need to be needed' is an embedded fear of abandonment somewhere in your subconscious, but you can transform any fear of abandonment into abundance. When we begin to practice boundary setting, we begin to understand we can no longer control or manipulate others, love or act out of feelings of guilt or obligation, or take on the resentment building responsibilities that aren't ours to take on in the first place. Having healthy boundaries is a form of self-love and self-respect.

The Boundary of Forgiveness

After my divorce, I was determined to hold onto my grudges. I did not want to let go of my pain; I wanted the other person to suffer as much as me. The anger fueled me. The smallest slight would set me off into a rage. The rage became depression. I was not able to move. I did not get out of bed. Time stood still.

I entered my therapist's office expressing "today's topic is forgiveness." (Therapists love when clients come prepared, and boy was I!) I was sick and tired of being told, 'you need to forgive!' And, "forgiveness is for you, not the other person." Not possible, I said. There was too much anger. Anger for the person who hurt me, anger for those who dared to tell me 'forgive." My therapist looked at me and said, "What does the word forgiveness mean to you?" Stumped, I sat in the chair and searched my mind for answers. My heart was unable to grasp the concept. We spent the hour tossing ideas back and forth. I left with no conclusion. I wanted inner clarity, where there was none.

For the next few weeks, the thought of forgiveness consumed me. I asked friends and family what it meant to them. I wanted someone to "tell me the answer so that I can wrap my head around it." I then realized this journey, this healing journey, was mine alone.

Forgiveness was a word I struggled with; I realize I grappled with it because my definition was different than how people define it today. I looked at today's meaning, as I understood it, not the dictionary version. Forgiveness was to pardon someone and *never forget what happened*. There it was. I could not accept today's meaning. I was 58 years old, and to change an essential principle or value I learned years ago was not going to happen, at least overnight.

Growing up, I was taught by family, teachers, church members that forgiveness comes instantly. It was a time when someone bonked you on the head out on the playground; the teacher called you over, somebody said they were sorry, the other person said, "Yeah, it's okay, no problem" and you ran off together and never thought about it again. *You let it go.*

Today's version of forgiveness is genuinely more of "I'll forgive you, but I will not forget what happened." So forgiveness is not necessarily reconciliation. (The adjective *reconciled* is from the verb *reconcile*, which is from the Latin root words *re*, meaning "again," and *conciliare*, meaning "to make friendly.") You can remember this if you think of a reconciled couple as once again being friendly to each other after a break-up. So, while reconciliation is about going back to a relationship, forgiveness is simply about letting it go from your end.

I set out to find a word I could relate to and understand that felt right to me. Weeks later, I walked back into my therapist's office and announced, "I have it; I know what forgiveness is to me." It is *acceptance*. Right now, I explained, it feels impossible to change my definition of forgiveness; it was a part of me. I had to find a word. I could a*ccept* what happened.

If I can *accept* something's happened, then I can let it go. I can *accept* bad things happen. I can *accept* loved ones can have awful behaviors and do terrible things. This word allowed *me* to accept yet not forget; it allowed me to understand what happened, not agree with or ignore it. This word allowed me to *let it go*. Acceptance was a beginning.

There is a season for sadness. There is a season for anger. Over time the pain can ease its grip. There is also a season for hope. The idea of forgiveness was too daunting, too big. This new word, acceptance, allowed me to transition into an integrative stage. I began to explore the possibilities and started to feel hopeful again. What was the next career phase? Will I trust again, will love come again? The options arrived with little fanfare or celebration; the pain eased with the same lackluster. It was subtle, until one day, I realized I was no longer affected. You will know when this happens because the pain of hearing someone's name no longer distresses you, you don't cringe at past hurts, the intense emotions have slipped away, seeing old photos no longer produce tears. Acceptance.

It is at this point that we understand to look at our lives as a whole. Experiences, good and bad, shape our lives. Acceptance, or forgiveness, does not happen overnight. It sneaks up on you. When you start to fill your life with possibilities, there is no time to wallow in pain or want revenge. The negative emotions will wear on you. The body will eventually feel the effects of negative energy. Do the work; go to therapy, yoga, exercise, and connect with others. "It's a decision we make," Mr. Rogers said, "to release a person from the feelings of anger we have toward them." Tell your story so many times so that it runs out of steam.

As a client said to me, "I'm not writing a new chapter in the book. I've decided my life is a book *series*. Today I'm writing a new book in an infinite series!" As she sat down, she said, "This is killing me! I'm over the relationship; I'm glad I'm no longer in it, it is over and yet something is missing, I feel angry with myself for staying so long. I want to start a new book." During our session, we discussed the feelings of anger, frustration, hopelessness, self-esteem when I asked, "What do you need right now?" Her eyes swelled with tears, "I need to learn to say I'm sorry, to me, and let this go; it's killing me."

I'm sorry. Two small words. Three syllables. One deep meaning. It seems simple enough. *I'm sorry* can be a game-changer for the better or make a situation worse. This simple phrase is often used for scenarios of which we have no control. "I'm sorry it's raining. I'm sorry the traffic was terrible." Neither of these situations is controllable. Women have become accustomed to saying *I'm sorry. FOR EVERYTHING.* The compulsion to apologize is less about remorse and more about anxiety. A University of Waterloo, Canada study found women apologize more than men and have a "lower threshold than men for what they consider offensive." The compulsive nature of apologizing stems from people-pleasing learned at an early age. It is a way to fill a gap when there is silence, and for some, it is about peace-keeping. Habitual apologizing may enforce a shame response to feeling wrong when punished. The obsessive apology can be pervasive in both our personal and professional lives. Women might stop believing in themselves; they might think, "I am less than."

Saying "I'm sorry," when done appropriately, is very powerful, compassionate, and restorative.

Taking responsibility is the best way to have an apology accepted. In every relationship - girlfriends, boyfriends, marriages, workmates, self - there will come a time when *I'm sorry* is crucial. Start by stating what behavior caused hurt feelings:

- I know going to the movies hurt your feelings...
- Throwing away your favorite tee shirt was a mistake...
- Laughing at you was terrible and hurtful...

Then state this wasn't your intention:

- I know going to the movies hurt your feelings. I didn't mean to hurt you. I made a mistake. I am sorry.

Do NOT defend yourself: I went because Mike asked me. I thought he needed a friend... Being defensive digs a hole deeper.

Do NOT ask for forgiveness. Forgiveness is up to the other person. Own your behavior, take responsibility, acknowledge the hurt caused; this is a sincere apology.

One of the exercises I have clients do is keep track of how many times "I'm sorry" happens during a day. Most people come back very surprised with the results. Together we create a list of mindful phrases to swap out for apologies.

Instead of saying "I'm sorry," to interrupt say:

- "Excuse me."
- "Pardon me."
- "I need to say something here,"
- "Do you mind if I interrupt?"
- "I have an idea that relates to what you just said,"
- "I'd like to add something to that,"
- "I'd like to add..."
- "I'd like to expand on that..."
- "I'd like to ask a question, please."
- "May I..."

Instead of saying sorry to keep the peace say:

- "I appreciate your work on this; I don't understand the reasoning behind this strategy switch."
- "What I am about to say might be controversial..."
- "Can we circle back...." (my favorite)
- "Let's look at this from another angle."

Instead of saying "sorry to complain," switch it to:
- "Thank you for listening..."
- "I appreciate being heard..."

Instead of apologizing in an email, consider saying:
- "Thank you for catching that...."
- "I appreciate you bringing this error to my attention....'
- "Thanks for flagging this issue for me..."

If you're running a little late, instead of saying sorry consider
- "Thank you for waiting for me..."
- "I'm grateful you were willing to wait!"

What to say instead of sorry for a loss or death?
- "I'm here whenever you need me." These simple word⋅ show the bereaved that they are not alone in **their** grief. ...
- "I wish you comfort and peace."...
- "I'm thinking of you."...
- "This must be very difficult."...
- "He/She was a wonderful person, and they will be missed."...
- "I love you, and I'm here."

Find A Way To Say 'Thank You'

Show concern without demeaning yourself by saying, "thank you." For example, if a project falls behind, skip the excuse ("I'm so sorry I don't have this to you yet") and exchange i⁺

with: "Thank you for your patience as we navigate this project. You will have it by Friday of next week." Take your power back by owning your situation, cutting out the sob story, and giving a simple thank you.

Practice Empathy Instead Of Giving A Sympathy 'Sorry'

Some people use "I'm sorry" to show sympathy. Instead, practice empathy by reflecting on what the other person might be feeling. For example, if someone shares a difficult story or experience, you might say, "That sounds like it was really hard for you." Sorry often conveys sympathy, which rarely makes the other person feel heard, valued, or better.

Ask For Constructive Feedback

Apologizing too much can come from having low self-esteem or feeling anxious. What better way to build your self-esteem than to get feedback? Ask, "Can you give me feedback on how I can do this differently?" Constructive feedback will support your success and increase self-confidence.

Every relationship, whether trying to mend harm or find closure, requires taking responsibility to heal. For some, it happens quickly, and for others, it is a long process. Often, we blame others for a rift or failure of a relationship. Doing so is part of the healing process. In time, if we take responsibility for personal feelings, thoughts, and behaviors; in other words, take some responsibility, we move forward in the healing process.

Chapter 7

Gratitude

I don't remember moving. I had not been out of bed for days. Darkness. I remember the darkness. It was not only around me, but it was in me. I was stuck. I had nothing to hold on to or grab. It was pervasive and covered me like a low lying fog on a winter's day. The blanket was heavy. Alone. Empty. Darkness, only darkness.

Each day starts with sunrise. It suggests the potential for the day ahead. It's about hope, it's about a new beginning, a unique chance. Sometimes after a storm, either literally or figuratively, we wake up and find the sun has risen, and all the possibilities lay ahead of us. This moment is a time for gratitude. Gratitude is about grounding, mindfulness, and appreciation for all that is good. It's about being able to push away anxiety or depressive thoughts and stay in the moment. We know, for a fact, it's nearly impossible for the brain to live in depression or anxiety while living a life of gratitude. For the past 10 to 12 years, I have studied gratitude, taken many courses on gratitude, and find it a fascinating practice.

My journey towards gratitude began years ago. I was challenged to do something that I do for my clients as well, which is to write ten things a day, bullet-point fashion for 30 days. I was given this challenge and thought, "Sure; I can do that for 30 days!" It's interesting to look back on those days because, in the very beginning, the first three days had nothing but "open eyes." That's right. Thirty times "open eyes." On the fourth day, it said, "Open eyes, put feet on floor." My mental state was dismal. It was a deep, dark depression, and I was trying to figure out how to get out of it. It was a time when several people, whom I loved and truly admired, had broken my trust. I had been lied to, manipulated, and was very heartbroken. I remember that time specifically because it was difficult to find anything worthy of gratitude.

During those days, when I literally could only open my eyes, I managed to rally for one person. If it was a day my son was coming by after school to hang out or do homework, I made sure to be up and dressed. I would put on the mask of 'everything is okay,' as long as he was in the house. But then I would go right back to that deep dark place. Interestingly enough, when I look at that journal, it starts adding different moments and situations for the next few weeks. There is a progression: a cup of coffee, clean sheets, a smile on my son's face, the sun shining, a pretty puffy dog-shaped cloud. Slowly but surely, I did come out of that deep, dark depression; it made me wonder, "Was it truly the gratitude journal?" I have come to decide that yes, that's what it was. It was the gratefulness that helped me put my feet on the ground again and see all that is around me.

Depression is looking into your rearview mirror and thinking about the past, the people who have hurt you, the negative things that have happened, the traumas, and experiences that were not pleasant. Anxiety is looking through the windshield of your car. It's what's out in front of you; it is the object or moment which is unknown. It is the future; it is vague and has no clarity.

Gratitude is about being in the moment and being mindful. It is knowing you are in the driver's seat and paying attention. I have a fabulous piece of art that reminds me of this daily. This painting is of someone, obviously in a dark, grey place. This person has little or no expression; the sense is heavy and oppressive; they are looking forward and gloomy.

Interestingly enough, they are standing in this amazing patch of wildflowers that are orange, yellow, pink, blue, purple, and green. The colors form a magical, rainbow-like carpet - it is gorgeous. As the observer, I want to scream, "Just look down; it's phenomenal, look down, and see the beauty that surrounds you!" This painting represents depression, not being able to see the good in your life. Gratefulness comes from seeking big and small details and showing appreciation. It is mindful of your surroundings, seeing where you are in the moment.

This practice, of writing down ten things a day for 30 days, is what my clients are encouraged to do. In the beginning, it's the big things like family and work, all of which are broad concepts. When you journal, be specific. The idea is to keep dwindling these ideas into smaller elements. What is it about the family? My three children. What is it about your three children? Well, it's about my son. What is it about your son? His laugh and giggle. Is it corny jokes, the flowers they bought, the cup of coffee in bed, or the prepared dinner? Why is the dog on the list? Did he do something silly to make you smile? Did he cuddle with you when you were tired? Is it the way he sleeps upside down? Is it his little pink tongue? Learn to take significant notions and find small details and be specific. The attitude of gratitude is living in the present, being mindful of the now.

Sharing gratitude is frequently part of the experience. Through the years, I have taken many classes, and occasionally we will share our journal entries. While one of my friends was reading his journal, I was amazed. I asked him to back up and read me the last three items. He read them to me again. "Thumbs" was the first one on the list. I said, "You have your thumbs in your gratitude journal?" He said, "Patty, do you not realize what thumbs do for us every single day?" He was right; thumbs turn pages, open milk cartons, pull on pants. You certainly can't have a thumb war without thumbs! He was in tune with the small things and appreciated them. He was mindful. He was living a life of gratitude.

Another way to introduce gratitude is by starting first thing in the morning. When waking up, immediately put one foot on the ground and say, "Thank you." Then put the other foot on the ground and say, "Thank you." If you are heading to the shower or getting coffee, it is possible to take 12 steps or more steps. Imagine twelve moments of appreciation by walking to the shower! What a fantastic practice and a magnificent way to start your day.

There is a science behind gratitude. Depression and gratitude do not co-exist. Depression diminishes when the brain is living in gratefulness. When a client comes into the office, whether it is for depression, I give them a journal and ask them to record ten gratitudes a day for thirty days.

Here is what I have noticed over the years about Gratitude:

- It nurtures positive emotions
- People feel alive
- It creates a deep connection with themselves
- They express more compassion and kindness
- People with gratitude have stronger immune systems
- People are aware of the abundance in life
- It makes you aware of the small pleasures
- It improves overall physical health
- It improves mental health and keeps you happier
- It promotes social interactions and relationships as it makes us friendlier
- It improves the quality of sleep
- It increases self-esteem
- It lessens depression

- Gratitude enhances empathy and reduces aggression
- It boosts resilience, so you are better able to cope with stress
- You are more likely to make healthier choices
- It makes you less self-centered and materialistic
- It eliminates negative emotions like envy, jealousy
- It helps you in your career
- It improves your focus in life
- It gives you peace of mind

The "attitude of gratitude," as I like to call it, is something we must train our brains to do. It is best done for thirty days because it takes that long to become a ritual, a habit. It takes practice. I suggest keeping a journal where you are most apt to pick it up: the nightstand, by your morning coffee, in your purse.

As I have studied the art of gratitude, my practice has changed over the years. Originally I wrote in a journal at night before I went to bed. It was suggested to make a mental note of what was appreciated as I went through my daily routine. This technique allowed me to be mindful all day long. Writing at night became simple.

Depression takes over the mind; it can be a struggle to be appreciative of anything. When someone is depressed, they find it difficult to look back over the day and find any gratitude. This adds to the depression! "Wow, I don't have anything to be grateful for." Remember, I had three days of "open eyes,' that is depressing! This practice helps teach us to live in the moment, to look down and see the flowers.

The Art of Handwriting

The next suggestion is about where to write. I suggest writing in a journal, as opposed to typing it on the computer or cell phone. The flow from your brain to the paper is one way the brain makes the connection through synapses. Also, the art of handwriting creates vibration. This vibration relaxes the mind and muscles in the body; it uses what we call the parasympathetic nervous system. This parasympathetic nervous system is the body's brake system and allows the body to calm down. When we give children paper and crayons or pens, they settle down. One, it occupies their brain and two, the vibration helps calm them down. Bring coloring books (calming) rather than phones (stimulates the brain) to your next dining experience.

Journaling, in this manner, can lead to measurable physical and mental health benefits. These benefits include everything from lower stress and fewer depression symptoms to improved immune function. Also, the process of writing involves pathways in the brain that go near or through parts that manage emotion. When stroking a keyboard or using our thumbs to write a note, the same part of the brain is not involved.

Several studies have verified handwritten notes help us relax. Taking a minute to slow down, be grateful, is a good habit in today's fast-paced world. It helps us use a wider variety of words as well as connect to our feelings and deepen our understanding of the universe around us.

A Gratitude Jar

Families can boost one another and have their specific practice as well. One idea is to create a gratitude jar. Place a big jar (or bowl) in an open area, say the kitchen, or an entrance hallway. Keep small pieces of paper, a pen, or a pencil ready. Each family member writes their gratitude down and places them in the jar. Then choose one night a week where everyone sits down, maybe it's Sunday night after dinner, and you go through the weeks' worth of gratitudes. Everybody pulls out a piece of paper from the jar and reads the gratitude. It might be their brother let them play basketball, or the sister took the dog for a walk, or both kids did the dishes, the kids got off to school on time, no arguing during homework, a freshly cooked meal. Maybe a sibling was heard saying something kind about them to a friend. Reading the gratitudes of each family member is affirming and fun for everybody.

No matter how big or small the thing you are grateful for, put it in a journal. Write about that great cup of coffee, your dog's tail, or thumbs! Gratitude stabilizes moods and helps people realize how many beautiful moments happen every day.

Gratitude is integral in making you have a more fulfilling life. It lets you see things in a positive light. It awakens the mind from negativity to positivity. It can improve the quality of life and help overcome negative emotions. Remember, negative feelings cannot co-exist with appreciation. Have an attitude of gratitude.

A New Vision

"I don't know who I am or what I want," she said. My client said she felt "lost." She lost all motivation to get up and to move in the morning. She had been busy taking care of everyone around her: her family, her workmates, neighbors, aging parents, everyone except herself.

When "stuck" is the main sentiment, a person might lack vision, a concept for what inspires or excites them. At this point, I suggest they do a vision board. One does not need to be crafty or clever to do a vision board. All that is needed is some old magazines, scissors, a glue stick, a poster board, and time. It would be best if you had a stress-free hour or two to put your board together. The only instruction given is to find photos or words that inspire or make you happy and position them in any way, shape, or form. Simply cut out the pictures and see what happens.

A few weeks later, my client returned with her vision board. She was beaming with pride with her newly acquired artwork. We talked about the process, and she was surprised at how much she enjoyed creating it. I asked if she learned anything. "No," she said matter of factly. "Describe your board for me," I asked. She lit up with excitement and told me every detail.

"What does all the water represent to you?

"That's where I feel the most whole, complete. That's where I was brought up. That's where my happy memories are. That's where I wish I was." "I didn't even notice it has all the water images." "Ahhh," I said.

"Who are these people?" I asked.

The answer revealed a truth. "I've isolated myself for so many years, and I want to be around community. I want to have neighbors; I want to be in touch with family members. I've cut myself off from everybody." Tears formed in the corners of her eyes. It was as if a curtain was being pulled back to reveal her inner, authentic essence.

While doing the vision board, my client enjoyed the experience, yet never 'processed it.' Telling me the details and what it meant to her was the beginning of a new journey. Motivation and excitement were in the air. With every word her story came alive; the "who" and "what" she wanted was clear. Although she had been stuck behind a large boulder, all she needed was a current to set her free to continue the journey.

Visualization is one of the most powerful mind exercises that you can do. It allows the imagination to be set free. **Your vision board should focus on how you want to feel**, not just on things that you want. Don't get me wrong, it's great to include the material stuff, too. However, the more your board focuses on how you want to feel, the more it will come to life. A vision board creates an emotional connection, which motivates you to work towards your goal. Once you put something on a vision board, you start to believe it is possible. It becomes more concrete and transparent in your mind, and it feels attainable. It helps you clarify your desires as you put them down. Feel free to modify your vision over time and reflect on it daily.

A vision board is powerful as it motivates you to turn your dreams into a tangible reality. Once you get a clear vision, it relaxes you and gives you direction. It makes you productive and hopeful. You become determined and self-confident with a vision board in front of you. It acts as a mental rehearsal and grows your desire for what you want. It gives you better intentions and allows you to work on your goals. I do vision boards because they provide clarity and define the purpose of bewildered people. My clients have all felt happier and more aware of their feelings once they have a vision board to guide them.

Traditions

His eyes were as wide and shiny as brand-new silver dollars. It was Thanksgiving and time for bed. When the door opened, Santa and his reindeer were dancing on my three-year-old son's bed. Full of wonder and excitement, this started our yearly tradition of Santa arriving a month before Christmas.

A tradition represents a part of a culture that is passed down from person to person or generation to generation. Traditions can be what binds a family or friends together. Some traditions are big and grand, while others are small, yet equally meaningful. Traditions are the glue for people. Not only does it give structure, but it also helps define a system that otherwise might be struggling. It helps everyone feel safe, like a warm blanket. Today's world is busy and often feels chaotic. Traditions or rituals allow us to feel settled, as if we belong and have a purpose. It helps us do what is so essential today - connect as human beings.

We live busy lives; there is basketball, soccer, ballet, flute, and gymnastic practices to attend. Business meetings. Family gatherings. With all of the activities, it is no wonder the family meal is nearly a thing of the past. For my family, the dinner table brought us together. The table was a place to share about the day, work, and life. It was a place to connect, where conversations might inspire the imagination to take flight or challenge a perspective. It is where we learned how to be curious about one another. It is where we learned to ask, "How was your day? What was fun today? What went right today? What didn't go so well today?" Simple questions that bind us together. Yes, I certainly remember the "eat your broccoli" meals, as well. Mostly I remember sharing or doing art projects with my brother while my mom made dinner. It was a simple time, and perhaps family dinners together may not seem like an important family tradition, but indeed, they are.

Okay, I know it can be challenging to juggle schedules and share a meal. Yes, it is 2019 and not 1950. But there are other ways to gather for 15-30 minutes 4-5 days a week. What about dessert at the end of a long day when everyone is back home? Offering root beer floats, popcorn, or ice cream is a perfect time to reconnect. For the little ones, how about sharing a bedtime story? It is about time, not the activity that is important to people. We know this: families who have this precious time together have less depression, less anxiety, and fewer eating disorders. During this time, a parent might recognize an issue that otherwise might have gone unnoticed. Traditions allow us to connect. They do create memories of our shared experiences.

While writing this book, the realization of how my own family traditions helped me communicate, connect, and celebrate with the people I love came to light. When my son was little, I bought new Christmas sheets for his bed. Every Thanksgiving, I snuck into his room and put on holiday sheets, and for years to come, he laid his head and dreamed of sugarplum fairies and the arrival of Santa. To this day (yep, he's 27!), if he's home on Thanksgiving, he still gets the early Christmas gift. Every year Santa stuffed the Christmas stockings; among the small gifts was a unique ornament to represent his year. One day these will adorn his own unique tree.

As my son grew up, there were new traditions added. Once the turkey was in the oven, he and I went to play hours of tennis. He did his best to beat his ol' mom! It was a sad day when, at the end of high school, he looked at me and said "too bad; this is our last time to play!" "What??? Are you dying, and I don't know about it?" He laughed and reminded me he was going off to college on a basketball scholarship, and we knew he would be playing basketball in a tournament somewhere. The sadness I felt knowing it would be a while before we played again was enormous. A sense of peace and calmness returned the day we played again; it was as if everything was in its place. There was the dying Easter Eggs and perhaps one of my favorites: carving pumpkins. When the kids grew out of this ritual, the parents carried it on as if not willing or wanting the tradition to die.

Another ceremony with my son began when he was in kindergarten. On the first and last day of every school year we would go for ice cream. Ice cream day allowed us to celebrate both the beginning and end of each year. These traditions grounded us. We created memories; time was shared; there was a sense of connection.

For these connections, celebrations, and memories, I am genuinely grateful. No one says it better than Melody Beattie:

"Gratitude unlocks the fullness of life. It turns what we have into enough, and more. It turns denial into acceptance, chaos to order, confusion to clarity. It can turn a meal into a feast, a house into a home, a stranger into a friend."

Conclusion

The river represents "us" when we are conscious of our oneness with the Universe and willing to trust the call of gravity, "going with the flow" of life without trying to force or manipulate it. The rock represents the past and our attachment to it; the rock symbolizes our resistance to change and fear of the unknown. This book, *Renew and Restore*, weaved stories from my life, as well as people I have met along the way. These stories demonstrate a need for transformation, a willingness to examine the past and prepare for the future. These pages offered an invitation to change the stories we tell ourselves to survive dysfunctional childhoods, traumas, friendships that ebb and flow, and to reframe them, so they empower us to move forward with the current.

Communication and Connection go hand in hand. Skills, such as not starting a sentence with "you" will encourage people to hear and be mindful of what is being communicated. All of us want to be seen, heard, and validated. The skills provided in the book will assist you in creating more profound, more meaningful connections within your community of family, friends, and business.

Safety, love, security, and a sense of belonging are needs we require to feel autonomous. These needs can be met when our environment, either personal or business, is a judgment-free zone. To accomplish this, change the "why" questions to the "whodunit" questions of what, where, who, and how. When this one word, *why* is substituted, the connections are much more heartfelt and meaningful.

You Should... Look how both of those together create a sense of shame! Remember to omit the first word "you," and that the word "*should*" generate a judgment, often stemming from our childhood. Try to be aware of how many times a day the word *should* is utilized. Once the "should" exercise is complete, hopefully, several items can be eliminated from your shame list! Once they move to a *goal,* the sense of ownership and empowerment strengthens your core belief, "I am...good enough, strong enough, deserving. I AM ENOUGH!"

An environment adopting active listening skills generates an atmosphere of safety, trust, new perspectives, and self control. Active listening requires us to stay mindful, not in our heads formulating our thoughts, hence creating a space where people can speak freely. Once we put our agenda of fixing something, or someone, or just the need to be heard aside for a few minutes, we send an open invitation for the person we are with to be seen, heard, validated.

Like a river that runs swiftly, technology is here to stay picking up speed every day; the need for boundaries is crucial. We have more ways to communicate with one another than any other time in history, yet we are the most disconnected from each other than ever before! Empathy is down 40 percent in this country. Empathy is, at its simplest, awareness of the feelings and emotions of other people, as if we can stand in their shoes. To have the ability to perceive, understand, and feel the *emotional* states of others, we must observe facial expressions, intonations, and have eye contact. Our fingers may be getting a workout, but our minds are going emotionally silent.

Just like the riverbank, healthy boundaries keep us safe from emotional pain. Coping skills used by children to keep them safe, especially in dysfunctional homes, turn maladaptive if not taught new strategies. Perhaps one needed to keep the peace, hold the family secret, not speak about emotions or did not have their emotional needs met. Other symptoms include having difficulty making decisions in a relationship, having trouble identifying your feelings, having a problem communicating in a relationship, valuing the approval of others more than valuing yourself, and lacking trust in yourself and having poor self-esteem. When we over-function in someone's life and under function in our own life, it is called codependency. What was once healthy coping skills as children are now considered as maladaptive symptoms: caretaking, peacekeeping, detachment, toxic positivity, people-pleasing, lack of boundaries, all of which are unhealthy ways to deal with life.

A way to manage the swift river water is through gratitude. It keeps us mindful of the present moment and is an emotion

expressing appreciation for what one has. It is a recognition
value independent of monetary worth. Spontaneou
generated from within, it is an affirmation of goodne
People who regularly practice gratitude by taking time
notice and reflect upon the things they're thankful
experience more positive emotions, feel more alive, sle
better, express more compassion and kindness, and ev
have stronger immune systems.

I am grateful to be with you here and now. This journ
expresses my belief in Mind, Body, and Spirit; meaning th
our well-being comes from not just physical health, but fro
mental health and spiritual health as well. I encourage you
do the exercises in the back of the book; they are simple, y
the results are wondrous. Please reach out to a profession
therapist for help if you need to. Reaching out is a sign
strength. Don't let stigma create self-doubt a
shame. Remember, stigma doesn't just come from othe
you may mistakenly believe that your condition is a sign
personal weakness or that you *should* be able to control
without help. Seeking therapy, educating yourself about yc
situation, and connecting with others who have mental hea
issues can help you gain self-esteem and overcor
destructive self-judgment. We believe in preventati
medicine; it's time to believe in preventative Mental Heal
Doing so, you will come to understand the words of Pla
"The unexamined life is the wasted life."

Together we are on a journey, a journey called life. There are 8,760 hours in a year, so give yourself the gift of self-exploration, time to find purpose beyond the roles you play. Be supportive and listen, truly listen to those around you. No matter where you are in your life, make time for yourself. Re-discover what gives you purpose, center yourself. Now it is your special time, just for you. Let yourself become the center of your life again. Let the world revolve around your needs for a change. Take the time to love yourself, and everything else will fall into place. Get back in touch with your strength and power. The circumstances of your life may be overwhelming you; take steps to connect with your own heart and soul, and suddenly you're back in touch with your center. You'll be amazed at how good you feel once that happens. May you communicate, connect, and celebrate your best self.

Bonus Chapter

Exercises

Should Exercise

At the top of a piece of paper, write Should/Shame. For several days write everything grand and small.

I SHOULD...

Go to the grocery store.

Own a 5-million-dollar house on the ocean.

Go to college.

After the list is comprehensive, take another piece of paper and write:

IF I REALLY WANTED TO, I COULD....

Break each of your items into both phases of the question:

1. DO I REALLY WANT TO:

   *Go to the grocery store?   No!

   *Own a 5-million-dollar house on the beach? YES!

   *Go to college? No!

   *Exercise? Yes!

2. Can I:

   *Go to the grocery store?   Yes!

*Own a 5-million-dollar house on the beach? No!

*Go to college? No!

*Exercise? Yes!

ANYTHING THAT HAS A SINGLE 'NO' REMOVE FROM THE LIST
REMOVE IT FROM THE SHAME LIST!

ANYTHING THAT HAS A 'YES' MOVE TO THE GOAL SHEET.

Goal Exercise

On your Goals Sheet, write the letters SMART going down the side of a paper:

S (specific)

M (measurable)

A (attainable)

R (realistic)

T (timebound)

Write down each item that had a 'yes' response and make sure it fits the criteria:

I do want to exercise and will do it every day.

This doesn't fit the SMART criteria, so break it down:

Specific: I will <u>walk</u> and <u>lift weights</u>

Measurable: I will walk <u>30 minutes every day</u>. I will lift free weights <u>three days a week</u>.

Attainable: No! Life will get in the way and *every* day is not possible (I may have to work late, there might be bad weather, vacations, illness,) <u>4 days a week</u> is attainable!

Realistic: Yes, it is now with the change.

Timebound: No! Six weeks is a good time and then the goal may be revised if necessary. The objective is to set you up for success!

It now reads:

I will walk 30 minutes a day, 4 days a week, for 6 weeks. I w
lift free weights 3 days a week for six weeks!

Well done!!! It is specific, measurable, attainable, realis
and timebound.

I Feel Exercise

This exercise helps get you in touch with your important feelings. Since they are how you feel, no one can tell you they "are wrong." This simple exercise helps state your feeling about a subject. Fill in the blanks:

I feel_____about _____.

Examples:

I feel <u>frustrated</u> about <u>the phone calls not being returned on time</u>.

I feel <u>overwhelmed</u> by <u>the documentation needed for the test</u>.

I feel <u>happy</u> about <u>going to the concert Friday.</u>

Most of us are not in the habit of stating our feelings and we use this sentence: I feel <u>because</u>… or I feel <u>Suzie</u>….. Neither "because" or "Suzie" is a feeling, so follow the guidelines to be accurate. This exercise will help you slow down enough to *think* and state how you feel!

Gratitude Journal Exercise

Write down, on paper, ten different things you are grateful for in a day. Do this each day for 30 days. This may be done in the morning or in the evening. Do not use your phone, or "think" about them; actually, write them down. The brain will remember them more intensely, and the body' parasympathetic nervous system will calm down due to the vibration of pen or pencil to the paper. Depression and gratitude do not coexist in the brain. The attitude of gratitude can:

- Nurture positive emotions
- Help people feel alive
- Create a deep connection with themselves
- Express more compassion and kindness
- People with gratitude have stronger immune system
- People are aware of the abundance in life
- Make you aware of the small pleasures

Gratitude Jar Exercise

Place a jar or bowl in an accessible place, along with paper and a pen. Every day write what you are appreciative of, and at the end of the week, read the gratitude notes at the end of a meal. This is fantastic for families big and small!

Vision Board Exercise

Visualization is one of the most powerful mind exercises you can do. It allows the imagination to be set free. **Your vision board should focus on how you want to feel**, not just on things that you want. Don't get me wrong, it's great to include the material stuff, too. However, the more your board focuses on how you want to feel, the more it will come to life. A vision board creates an emotional connection, which motivates you to work towards your goal. Once you put something on a vision board, you start to believe it is possible. It becomes more concrete and transparent in your mind, and it feels attainable. It helps you clarify your desires as you put them down. Feel free to modify your vision over time and reflect on it daily.

One does not need to be crafty or clever to do a vision board. You will need old magazines, scissors, a glue stick, a poster board, and time. It would be best if you had a stress-free hour or two to put your board together. The only instruction given is to find photos or words that inspire or make you happy and position them in any way, shape, or form. Simply cut out the pictures and see what happens.

Boundaries Exercise

Believing that your needs, preferences, and opinions are just as important as everyone else's is the first step in boundary setting. Make a list of:

- Five things you enjoy doing
- Five things you *don't* enjoy doing
- Five values that are highly important to you (e.g., family, friends, career, free time, physical activity, nature, etc.)
- Five types of behavior that you will not tolerate in yourself or others.

You now have a good starting point for how and where to set boundaries that are meaningful to you. For example, if you love spending time with family but get very annoyed when family members arrive late to planned activities, there's a boundary you can set. You may not be able to control their punctuality, but you can communicate to them in a firm but polite way how you feel about it and ask them to cooperate.

Renew and Restore

About the Author

Patty Mohler, MS, LMHC, is a highly renowned Keynote Speaker, Behavioral Transformation Consultant, Communications Accelerator, and a Licensed Mental Health Counselor. Owner and Founder of Patty Mohler Counseling and Renew and Restore, Patty is a specialist in cultivating effective communication to build long-lasting, deep, and meaningful (personal and professional) relationships. A graduate from the University of North Florida (CACREP accredited), Patty earned a Master in Clinical Mental Health Counseling. She is the past President of Chi Sigma Iota (CSI) and was selected to the Mayor's Victims Assistance Advocacy Counsel (VAAC). Highly sought-after as a respected leader in her industry, Patty has appeared as a Keynote Speaker at PACT (Prevention Coalition of St. John's County); Behavior Therapist at St. Vincent's Bariatric Program; Dean Ornish Heart Reversal

Program at St. Vincent's; and Lead Therapist/Lecturer a American Foundation for Suicide Prevention (AFSP) Celebrating Possibilities, and Deutsche Bank.

Patty offers diverse, customized programs, including mastermind groups, workshops, lunch and learns, retreats and speaking for businesses, professional groups, and events

To learn how Patty can help you better communicate connect, and celebrate, check out her women's retreat *Renew and Restore: A Weekend to Explore and Connect to Your Best Self* at **RenewRestoreRetreat.com.**

You may also contact her at:

Patty@pattymohlercounseling.com

Special Acknowledgments

Photo Credit:
Julie Ryan Photographers
Julie@julieryanphotography.com

Makeup Credit:
Carrie Wilson Makeup
Carrie@carriewilsonmakeup.com

Hair Credit:
Terre Bulan
Apres Salon Jacksonville

Renew and Restore

Made in the USA
Middletown, DE
28 January 2020